Verdi

Genn.º 1900

Verdi

CHARLES OSBORNE

M

Other books by Charles Osborne include

The Complete Operas of Verdi
Letters of Giuseppe Verdi (*ed. and trans.*)
The Concert Song Companion
Wagner and His World

to Ken Thomson

In the theatre, 'long' is synonymous with 'boring',
and the boring is the worst of all styles — Verdi to
Antonio Somma

First published 1978 by
MACMILLAN LONDON LIMITED
London and Basingstoke

Associated companies in Delhi, Dublin,
Hong Kong, Johannesburg, Lagos, Melbourne,
New York, Singapore and Tokyo

Printed in Hong Kong

British Library Cataloguing in Publication Data
Osborne, Charles, b. 1927
    Verdi.
    1. Verdi, Giuseppe   2. Composers, Italian –
    Biography
    782.1'092'4   ML410.V4

ISBN 0-333-21483-8

Contents

1 The Early Years: Oberto to Nabucco

Two great composers of opera were born in 1813: Giuseppe Verdi, in the Duchy of Parma, then part of Napoleon's empire but soon to become Austrian; and Richard Wagner, in Saxony, where Napoleon's troops were busy fighting the combined forces of Russia and Prussia. Both men were to become actively engaged in revolutionary movements; indeed politics would strongly influence their choice of operatic subject and even their music. Both were innovatory artists, geniuses who completely changed the face of opera both in and beyond their own countries. Verdi's achievement was to humanize Italian opera, to transform it from show business to art; Wagner's path lay in a different direction: by what might be thought of as a dehumanizing process, he led German opera back to the realm of myth and the old Northern gods. Opera, potentially the highest of art forms, combining as it does elements of them all, was flexible enough to be extended in opposite directions by the genius of these two men.

The backgrounds of the two composers were vastly different. Wagner was born into a middle-class family with an interest in the arts, but Verdi's father, the innkeeper at Le Roncole, a small village three miles from Busseto and about twelve miles from Parma, was a semi-literate peasant. Carlo and Luigia Verdi had two children: the younger, a mentally retarded girl named Giuseppa, died at the age of seventeen, while the elder, Giuseppe, born on 10 October 1813, lived to become Italy's greatest composer. At the time of Giuseppe Verdi's birth, France and Austria were engaged in fighting over possession of northern Italy; a

The house in which Verdi was born in the village of Le Roncole.

united and independent Italy did not come into existence until much later in the nineteenth century, and life for the farming community in the country around Parma cannot have been easy. The story is told that, in the year after Giuseppe's birth, Russian cossacks came marauding through the village in search of the retreating French, killing and looting indiscriminately, and that Luigia Verdi saved the life of her infant son by hiding with him in the church just opposite the inn.

Though there was no musical talent in his family, Giuseppe took early and naturally to music, sufficiently so for his father to buy him a second-hand, broken-down spinet which was repaired by a neighbour, and upon which the boy first began to learn music. To begin with he was given lessons by the church organist, but by the time he was twelve the young Verdi had himself become the church organist. His father agreed to allow him to continue his musical tuition in Busseto, and the lad went to live there, attending a school where music was part of the curriculum and having additional lessons from Ferdinando Provesi, head of the local music school and organist of the cathedral. A Busseto merchant, Antonio Barezzi, befriended Giuseppe, gave him lodgings in his house and generally behaved *in loco parentis*. Every Sunday, Giuseppe walked to and from Le Roncole, not only to see his father and mother but also because he was still required to play the organ for the Sunday services.

When Verdi reached the age of sixteen, his benefactor Barezzi realized that he ought to be given an opportunity to continue his musical studies at a higher level than could be offered in Busseto. He advised the boy's father upon an application to a local charitable institution for a

grant towards the expense of enrolling him at the Milan Conservatorium. The application was successful, and Barezzi supplemented the grant out of his own pocket. So, in 1832, Verdi went to Milan and presented himself at the Conservatorium for examination. By now he was eighteen, four years older than the official age limit, and the board of examiners did not think so highly of his abilities that they were willing to bend the rules in his favour. However, one of the examiners advised Verdi to study privately with Vincenzo Lavigna, chief conductor at La Scala Opera House and reputed to be a first-rate teacher. Verdi was accepted by Lavigna and studied under him in Milan for two years. He proved to be a brilliant student, and was soon composing works which he sent back to Busseto for performance by the local philharmonic society.

Left: The Viennese pianoforte on which the young Verdi composed in Barezzi's house.
Right: The church organ at Le Roncole.
Below: The library of the Monte di Pietà di Busseto.

The young Verdi with a pupil, who may be Margherita Barezzi.

Invited to take a rehearsal of Haydn's oratorio, *The Creation*, when the conductor had failed to arrive, Verdi did so with such success that he was allowed to conduct the public performance at the Teatro dei Filodrammatici. This eventually led to his being given the opportunity to compose an opera for the theatre. Whether the opera which Verdi began to write was called *Rocester* (in which case the manuscript has been lost) or whether it is the one which was eventually to be produced as *Oberto* is not known. In 1836 the twenty-three-year-old composer returned to Busseto to apply for the post of cathedral organist, but he was unsuccessful in this. He married Margherita, the daughter of his benefactor Barezzi, and returned to Milan with his wife, having completed work on

10

an opera, *Oberto*, whose libretto had been written by Antonio Piazza, a Milanese journalist, and revised by Temistocle Solera, a young poet and composer. The Teatro dei Filodrammatici had by now changed hands, but *Oberto* was accepted by Bartolomeo Merelli, the impresario of La Scala, and a cast was assembled which included the soprano Giuseppina Strepponi, Merelli's mistress. The production had to be postponed when the tenor became ill, and it was largely due to Strepponi's enthusiasm for the opera that it was at last staged in the following year, 1839, though she herself was not free at that time to take part in it. By the time of the opera's première, tragedy had struck the Verdi household. Margherita had given birth to two children: a girl, Virginia, in 1837, and a boy, Icilio, the following year. A month after the

The road which Verdi walked as a child when, lodging in Busseto, he returned to Le Roncole to visit his parents and play the organ.

boy was born, the girl died; fifteen months later, a few weeks before the first night of *Oberto*, the boy died.

Oberto, a romantic opera set in thirteenth-century Italy, is no blazing masterpiece, but it combines an almost Bellinian delicacy and melodic fecundity with a distinctly un-Bellinian vigorous energy. The opera was sufficiently original for the critics to approve of it, and was well received by its first audience; it was performed fourteen times during the autumn season of 1839, and was bought for publication by the firm of Ricordi, who were to remain Verdi's principal publishers throughout his lifetime. The Scala impresario Merelli offered Verdi a contract to compose a further three operas during the following two years, and *Oberto* began to be asked for by other Italian opera houses. In the two years immediately following its première it was produced in Turin, Genoa and Naples. The young composer's

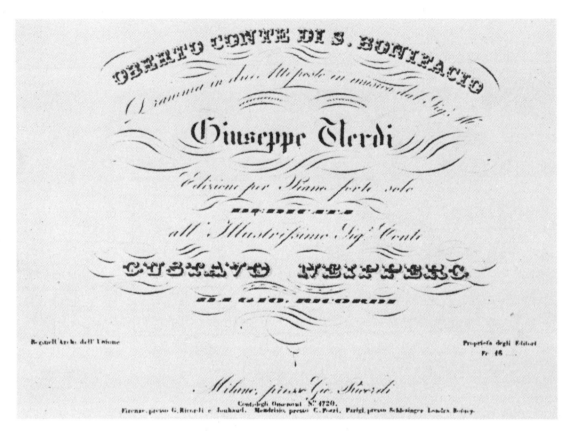

Left: Margherita Barezzi, Verdi's first wife.
Above: Cover of the piano score of Oberto, *Verdi's first opera.*

career had, it seemed, got off to a good start.

Having decided that he needed a comic opera (*opera buffa*) for the following autumn season, Merelli offered Verdi several libretti. Verdi did not think highly of any of them, but finally chose *Il finto Stanislao* (The False Stanislaus) which the well-known librettist Felice Romani had written for another composer, Adalbert Gyrowetz, more than twenty years earlier. The libretto was given a new title, *Un giorno di regno* (A One-Day Reign), and Verdi began work on the opera in February 1840. A few days later he became ill and was confined to his bed with an attack of angina. His wife Margherita nursed him devotedly, and after some days he felt well enough to resume work. But the March quarter-day was approaching, and he suddenly realized he had not sufficient money to pay the rent of their apartment. The mail from Milan to Busseto went only twice a week so there was not sufficient time to appeal to his father-in-law. Seeing his distress, Verdi's wife went out and pawned what little jewellery she possessed.

In June, while Verdi was still composing his comic opera, Margherita fell seriously ill with encephalitis, and on 18 June she died. Her father arrived in Milan just in time to be with her; after the funeral Verdi, in a state of black despair, returned to Busseto with Barezzi, having asked the impresario Merelli to release him from his contract. But Merelli wisely refused to allow his young composer to submerge himself in his grief. He insisted that he should persevere with the until his veritable metamorphosis of the genre with *Falstaff* more than half a century later, but his early comic opera has great charm and melodic facility. In later years his mastery of the orchestra was to make the scoring of *Un giorno di regno* sound rather primitive, with its equation of high spirits with a liberal use of the percussion instruments. But his vocal writing already displayed assurance and style, and modern revivals of *Un giorno di regno* at Bregenz and elsewhere have revealed it to be as entertaining a comedy as many of Donizetti's, though it falls far short of that composer's two comic masterpieces, *L'elisir d'amore* and *Don Pasquale*.

Many years later, Verdi dictated his recollections of his early years for use in a biography by the French critic Arthur Pougin. Here is his own account of the events immediately following the

Above: The distinguished librettist Felice Romani, who wrote the libretto of Un giorno di regno, *Verdi's second opera.*

Below: Passport issued to Verdi in 1832 (on the left is a description of his features).
Right: Verdi at the age of twenty-nine.

opera, and so Verdi returned to Milan, to the house in which his wife had died, and forced himself to continue composing his comic opera. In the circumstances it seems hardly surprising that the première of *Un giorno di regno* at La Scala on 5 September 1840 should have been an unmitigated disaster. The press was cruelly hostile, but what wounded Verdi most was the reaction of the audience, which booed and hissed the first performance. There was no second performance: instead, Merelli hastily revived *Oberto*. Embittered by the failure of the public to make any allowance for the circumstances in which he had written the opera, Verdi swore he would never compose again.

When one considers not only the tragic death of his wife while he was at work on the opera, but also the composer's own temperament, nervous and inclined towards melancholy, it is surprising that *Un giorno di regno* should be so enjoyable a work. Verdi did not attempt *opera buffa* again

failure of *Un giorno di regno*, and of how he came to compose his third opera and the first by which he became known beyond Italy.

Un giorno di regno did not succeed. A share of the want of success certainly belongs to the music, but part must also be attributed to the performance. My soul rent by the misfortunes which had overwhelmed me, my spirit soured by the failure of my opera, I persuaded myself that I should no longer find consolation in art, and formed the resolution to compose no more! I even wrote to Signor Pasetti (who since the fiasco of *Un giorno di regno* had shown no signs of life) to beg him to obtain from Merelli the cancellation of my contract.

Merelli sent for me and treated me as a capricious child. He would not allow me to become disgusted with art on account of one failure, etc., etc. But I held to my point so firmly that Merelli finished by returning to me my agreement, saying: 'Listen, Verdi, I cannot make you write by force. My confidence in you is not lessened. Who knows but that one day you may decide to take up your pen again? In that case, it will be enough for you to give me notice two months before the beginning of a season, and I promise that the opera which you bring me shall be put on the stage.'

I thanked him; but these words did not have the effect of making me reconsider my determination, and I went away.

I took up residence in Milan, near to the Corsia de' Servi. I was out of spirits, and thought no more of music, when one winter evening, coming out of the Cristoforis gallery, I found myself face to face with Merelli, who was going to the theatre. It was snowing great flakes, and Merelli, drawing my arm in his, induced me to accompany him as far as his office at La Scala. We chatted on the way, and he told me that he was in difficulties for a new opera which he had to bring out. He had engaged Nicolai to write this opera, but he was not satisfied with the libretto.

'Fancy,' said Merelli, 'a libretto by Solera, superb!!... magnificent!!... extraordinary!!... splendid dramatic situations, full of interest, fine poetry!... but this obstinate Nicolai will not hear of it, and declares that it is an impossible libretto!... I would give my head to find another immediately.'

'... I will get you out of the difficulty,' said I at once. 'Did you not have *Il proscritto* written for me? I have not composed a note of it; I put it at your disposal.'

'... Oh! bravo! This is a piece of luck.'

Thus conversing we had arrived at the theatre. Merelli called Bassi, who was at the same time poet, stage manager, librarian, régisseur, etc., etc., and told him to look at once among the archives to try and find a manuscript of *Il proscritto*. As a matter of fact, he did find it. But at the same moment, Merelli took another manuscript, and showing it to me, cried out:

'... Stop; here is the libretto of Solera's. So fine a subject, and to refuse it! Take it; read it!'

'... What the deuce do you want me to do with it? I have no wish to read libretti.'

'... Well, I suppose it will not hurt you! Read it, and then bring it back to me.'

And he put it into my hands. It was a large paper book, written in big letters, as was the custom then. I rolled it up, and taking leave of Merelli, made my way to my lodging.

As I walked, I felt myself seized with a kind of undefinable uneasiness; a profound sadness, a genuine anguish, took possession of my heart. I went into my room, and with an impatient gesture I threw the manuscript on the table, and remained standing before it. In falling on the table, it had opened by itself; without knowing how, my eyes fixed on a page which was before me, and on this verse:

'Va, pensiero, sull' ali dorate.'

I ran through the following verses, and was much impressed by them, the more so that they formed almost a paraphrase of the Bible, the reading of which was always dear to me.

I read first one fragment, then another, but, firm in my resolution to compose no more, I tried to command myself. I shut the book, and went to bed. But bah! *Nabucco* ran in my head; I could not sleep. I got up and read the libretto, not once, but twice, three times, so that in the morning I was able to say that I knew Solera's poem by heart, from one end to the other.

In spite of all this, I felt no disposition to change my determination, and during the day

Bartolomeo Merelli, the impresario of La Scala, Milan, who accepted Verdi's first opera.

16

I went back to the theatre to return the manuscript to Merelli.

'Oh!' said he, 'isn't it fine?'

'Very fine.'

'Well, set it to music.'

'Not at all! I will have nothing to do with it.'

'Set it to music, I say; set it to music.'

And with these words he took the libretto, rammed it into the pocket of my overcoat, took me by the shoulders, and not only pushed me roughly out of his office, but shut the door in my face and locked himself in.

What was I to do?

I returned home with *Nabucco* in my pocket. One day one verse, one day another, one time a note, another time a phrase, and little by little the opera was written.

It was the autumn of 1841, and recalling Merelli's promise, I called on him to announce that *Nabucco* was finished, and that consequently it might be presented in the next season of Carnival and Lent.

Giorgio Ronconi (baritone), who sang the title-role in the first production of Nabucco.

Merelli declared that he was ready to hold his promise; but at the same time he pointed out to me that it would be impossible for him to give my work in the next season, because the pieces were already arranged, and that he had made choice of three new operas by well-known composers. To give a fourth by an author who was making almost his first appearance was dangerous for everyone concerned, and especially for me. It would therefore be most convenient, as he thought, to wait till the spring, a time when he was under no obligations, and he assured me that he would engage good artists. But I declined—either during the Carnival, or not at all. For that I had good reasons, for it was not possible to find two artists more suited to my work than Signora Strepponi and Ronconi, who I knew were engaged, and on whom I founded great hopes.

Merelli, with every wish to please me, was not in the wrong from a director's point of view. Four new operas in a single season was a tremendous risk to run. But, on the other hand, I had on my side good artistic arguments, which favoured my view of the question. In short, in the midst of yes and no, of arguments, of perplexity, of half-promises, the *cartellone* of La Scala was published, and *Nabucco* was not announced in it.

I was young; my blood was warm. I wrote to Merelli a foolish letter, in which I let off all my anger; and I confess that no sooner was the letter sent than I felt a certain remorse, fearing that in consequence I had destroyed all my hopes.

Merelli sent for me, and when he saw me, said, roughly: 'Is this the way to write to a friend? ... But no matter! you are right, and we will give *Nabucco*. But you must bear this in mind: I have very heavy expenses to meet for the other new operas; consequently, I shall be able to make neither scenery nor costumes for *Nabucco*, so that you will have to be satisfied with the best arrangement that can be made with what can be found in stock.'

I agreed to all, so anxious was I that my opera should be given; and I saw a new *cartellone* appear, on which I was able at last to read NABUCCO!

Here I call to mind an amusing scene which I had had a short time previously with Solera. In the third act he had included a little love duet between Fenena and Ismaele; this duet did not

The opening of the chorus 'Va, pensiero' from the original score of Nabucco.

please me; it interrupted the action, and seemed to me to diminish the Biblical grandeur which characterized the subject. One morning when Solera was with me, I mentioned this to him; but he would not allow it, because he would have had to revise a work already out of hand. We each discussed our reasons; I held to mine, and he to his. At last he asked me what I wanted in the place of the duet, and I suggested to him the idea of the prophecy of Zacharias. This idea struck him as not bad; for all that he was full of '*ifs*' and '*buts*', up to the moment when he told me that he would think it over, and that he would write the scene shortly. This did not suit me at all; knowing him well, I was certain that days and days would slip away before Solera brought himself to the point of writing a single

line. So I shut the door, put the key in my pocket, and half serious and half in joke, I said to Solera: 'You don't leave this room till you have written the prophecy. Here is a Bible; you will find the words there; all you have to do is to put them into verse.' Solera, who was of rather a hasty nature, did not take it in very good part. A spark of anger glittered in his eyes; I went through an unpleasant moment, for he was a sort of Colossus, who would soon have had the best of my weak frame. But all of a sudden he sat down quietly; and a quarter of an hour after, the prophecy was written.

At last, towards the end of February 1842, the rehearsals of *Nabucco* began, and twelve days after the first rehearsal at the pianoforte, the first performance, which was given on 9 March, took place. I had for interpreters Mesdames Strepponi and Bellinzaghi, with Ronconi, Miraglia and Derivis.

With this work my artistic career really began; and if I had to struggle against numerous difficulties, it is none the less certain that *Nabucco* was born under a happy star, for everything which might have injured it turned to its advantage. In fact, I wrote Merelli a furious letter, as a consequence of which it seemed quite likely that the impresario would send the young maestro to the devil, and the contrary happened; the threadbare costumes, rearranged skilfully, became splendid; the old scenery, retouched by the painter Perroni, produced an extraordinary effect, and especially the first scene, which represented the Temple, aroused so much enthusiasm that the public clapped their hands for at least ten minutes; at the full rehearsal it had not been decided when, nor how, the military band was to enter; the chief, Tutsch, was much troubled; I gave him the cue, and at the first performance the band came on the stage with such precision on the crescendo, that the public broke out in applause.

It does not do, however, always to trust to lucky stars. Experience has shown me the truth of our proverb, 'Fidarsi è bene, ma non fidarsi è meglio'—'To trust is good; to mistrust is better'.

Nabucco was a success right from the beginning. The first-night audience was wildly enthusiastic, and insisted on a repeat of the nostalgic chorus 'Va, pensiero', in which the captive Jews in Babylon sing of their homeland. Governed by Austrians, it was easy for the Milanese to identify themselves with the Jews of the Old Testament, and so with this chorus Verdi immediately and inadvertently became identified with the Risorgimento, the movement for a united and free Italy. In the years immediately following its première, *Nabucco* was performed throughout Europe and in the Americas. In Milan it continued to be enthusiastically received, season after season.

Solera's libretto was based on the Old Testament references to the Babylonian Emperor Nebuchadnezzar, though he took his plot from a French play without bothering to acknowledge the fact. Upon it Verdi wrote a fine though uneven opera, the earliest of his works still to hold its place in the repertoire. In *Nabucco* he adds his own freshness, vigour and emotional intensity to Bellinian grace and Donizettian flair. It is also the first of his operas to possess a significance of its own, above and beyond the sum of its frequently superb components: the chorus already mentioned, Abigaille's aria in Act II whose sinuous line and elegant figuration recall Bellini's 'Casta diva' in *Norma*, Zaccaria's solemn prayer 'Tu sul labbro', and Nabucco's remarkable solo scene at the beginning of Act IV. Throughout the opera, the choruses are splendid, embracing a wide range of feeling. The orchestra, too, is used with a greater freedom and expressiveness than in the two earlier operas. Especially effective are the various combinations of woodwind used to produce that dark, melancholy sound which is so distinctive a feature of Verdi's mature orchestration. The sense of exile and loss which pervades the opera is real and affecting. No less so are the main characters: the neurotic Nabucco, in some ways an adumbration of the Macbeth Verdi was to create five years later, and the cruel, single-minded Abigaille, clearly an ancestor of Lady Macbeth.

2 The 'Galley Years' I:
I Lombardi to Attila

Verdi was right in saying that his artistic career really began with *Nabucco*. However, the success of that opera had the immediate effect of catapulting him into the commercial operatic world which required composers to produce opera after opera in quick succession. He was never to acquire the manic facility which enabled Donizetti to write an opera in a few days, but every year, between *Nabucco* in 1842 and *Rigoletto* in 1851, he composed at least one opera, and sometimes two. He was later to refer to this period as his 'years in the galleys', and he must often have felt like a galley slave, racing to fulfil his commitments. There is no doubt that the pace he was obliged to keep up resulted in his operas containing here and there pages of mechanically contrived music. But the really dull moments are rare; these works display an unusual combination of nervous energy and brooding romanticism which distinguishes them from the operas being produced by most other composers of the time.

The success of *Nabucco* also opened for Verdi the doors to Milanese society. Among the people he met were the Maffeis, who were to become his friends for life. Andrea Maffei, poet and translator, was the husband of the Countess Clara Maffei whose literary and political salon was the most important in Milan. Another salon which Verdi frequented was that of Giuseppina Appiani, whose chief interest was in music and musicians. Bellini had composed *La sonnambula* while a guest in her house, and Donizetti had composed *Linda di Chamounix*. But now Bellini was dead, Donizetti had gone to Vienna to become composer to the Austrian Emperor, and Verdi was the new hero of the moment. Life was not all socializing for the twenty-nine-year-old composer, how-

ever, for Merelli had asked him for another opera, immediately after the triumphant success of *Nabucco*, and had told him he could name his own terms. Verdi very sensibly consulted the soprano Giuseppina Strepponi, who had helped *Oberto* on to the stage and had sung in *Nabucco*, and Strepponi suggested he should ask for the same fee as Bellini had received for *Norma* eleven years earlier. Merelli agreed, and Verdi set to work, again with Solera as librettist.

The subject chosen was *I Lombardi alla prima crociata* (The Lombards at the First Crusade), a dramatic poem by Tommaso Grossi which had been published in Milan some sixteen years earlier, and which wove a fictional story into the events of the Crusade. When Solera's libretto was submitted to the censors, exception was taken to a scene in which the dying hero is baptized. To portray the sacrament of baptism was considered sacrilegious by the Archbishop of Milan, upon whose instructions the Chief of Police attempted to persuade Verdi and Solera to delete it. When he summoned Verdi to appear, the composer refused. Fearing that the first-night audience would riot if the baptism was not allowed, the unhappy Chief of Police agreed to allow the opera to proceed as planned, provided that, in another scene, the words 'Ave Maria' were changed to 'Salve Maria'. Acting on Verdi's behalf, Merelli agreed to this pointless substitution, and *I Lombardi* was performed at La Scala on 11 February 1843. A capacity audience, many of whom had queued for several hours to obtain seats, applauded vociferously, and a police rule that there should be no encores was broken time and time again. From the very beginning of the opera, the Milanese audience identified themselves with

their eleventh-century ancestors, and the Saracens with nineteenth-century Austrians. In the final act, when the Lombards, about to capture Jerusalem from the Saracens, cheered themselves on with the words 'La Santa Terra oggi nostra sarà' (Today the Holy Land will be ours) a number of people spontaneously shouted 'Sì', which provoked an outburst of cheering. Again, without having consciously intended to do so, Verdi had allied himself with the aspirations of his audience, and had written music which stirred their patriotic feelings. (Nevertheless, his Italian patriotism

Left: Countess Clara Maffei, who was a lifelong friend of Verdi.
Below: Title-page of the first edition of the libretto of I Lombardi.

I LOMBARDI
ALLA PRIMA CROCIATA

DRAMMA LIRICO
DI TEMISTOCLE SOLERA

POSTO IN MUSICA
DAL SIG. MAESTRO GIUSEPPE VERDI

DA RAPPRESENTARSI
NELL' I. R. TEATRO ALLA SCALA
IL CARNEVALE MDCCCXLIII.

Milano

PER GASPARE TRUFFI
MDCCCXLIII

did not prevent him some weeks later from travelling to Vienna to conduct his *Nabucco*.)

I Lombardi is a typical early Verdi opera in the sense that music of great melodic beauty and creative energy alternates with much that is so brutally offhand as to be almost comical. The chorus of ruffians in the opening scene is the kind of thing that Gilbert and Sullivan satirized in the pirates' chorus 'With cat-like tread' in *The Pirates of Penzance*, the *piano* phrases of the ruffians punctuated by *forte* chords from an orchestra apparently determined to foil their attempts at stealth. But, in the following scene, Giselda's beautiful prayer 'Salve Maria' is scored with delicacy and imagination, especially the section in which only flute and clarinet accompany the voice. Those pieces which are either perfunctory or vacuous or both—a chorus here, a cabaletta there—are more than outweighed by really superb writing, for the orchestra as much as for the voices. The ignorant gibe that, until *Aida*, Verdi wrote nothing but barrel-organ tunes to skeletal accompaniments which merely marked the rhythm is demonstrably absurd. At his best the young Verdi wrote for his orchestra with the imagination and skill of a Berlioz, and with a mastery of effect gained by the most economical means. Though some of the music in *I Lombardi* does no more than match the crudity of its librettist's historical imagination, the finest numbers are possessed of that melodic beauty and creative energy which were, in due course, to be recognized as Verdian characteristics.

Verdi had been fortunate in having his first four operas produced at La Scala, Milan, Italy's leading opera house. His next commission came from another theatre, the almost equally prestigious Teatro la Fenice in Venice. The director of the theatre, Count Carlo Mocenigo, offered to open his 1843–4 season with *I Lombardi*, to be conducted by Verdi, who would also produce a new opera for performance the following month. Verdi agreed in principle, and by the end of May terms

23

had been arranged. The choice of a subject took longer: Verdi rejected several suggestions made by Mocenigo, including Rienzi (the subject of an opera by Wagner performed the previous year in Dresden, though Verdi is hardly likely to have been aware of this, since Wagner's fame had not yet spread beyond Germany), Catherine Howard, and Shakespeare's *King Lear*.

For his Venice opera Verdi finally agreed on Victor Hugo's play *Hernani*, which had been produced in Paris at the Comédie Française thirteen years earlier. (Some months after its Paris première, Bellini undertook to compose an opera on *Hernani*, and sketched five musical numbers before abandoning the project and using up most of the music in *Norma* and other operas.) Verdi himself drafted the synopsis of a libretto, and it was agreed that Francesco Maria Piave, a Venetian poet attached to the Fenice, should turn it into dramatic verse.

A scene from the London production of I Lombardi, *Her Majesty's Theatre, 1846.*

Verdi, meanwhile, was rehearsing *I Lombardi*, which opened the Fenice's season on 26 December. At one o'clock the next morning, the composer wrote frankly to his friend Giuseppina Appiani in Milan:

> You are impatient to hear the news of *I Lombardi*, so I hasten to send it to you: it's not a quarter of an hour since the curtain fell.
> *I Lombardi* was a great fiasco, one of the really classic fiascos. Everything was disapproved of, or merely tolerated, with the exception of the cabaletta of the vision. That is the simple truth which I relate to you with neither pleasure nor sorrow.

Undaunted, Verdi proceeded to compose his new opera, whose Italian title was *Ernani*. He bullied his amiable librettist Piave, and fought successful battles with the censoring authorities.

But he encountered a more serious difficulty when he proposed to have one of his characters bring a hunting horn on stage in the final scene, for the board of management of the Fenice took the view that this would be an affront to the dignity of their distinguished theatre. Verdi won that battle, too, and even held out successfully against his prima donna, Sophie Loewe, who disapproved of his plan to end the opera with a trio. In her opinion, a solo cabaletta for herself would bring the curtain down much more effectively, and behind the composer's back she had ordered Piave to write the verses for such a cabaletta. Accustomed to taking orders, Piave wrote the verses, only to be told by Verdi to throw them away. Sophie Loewe gave in, but with great reluctance.

Ernani was given its first performance on 9 *Sophie Loewe* (*soprano*), *the first Elvira.*

March 1844, and the following day Verdi wrote again to Giuseppina Appiani:

Ernani, performed last night, was a pleasant enough success. If I had had singers who were, I won't say sublime, but at least able to sing in tune, it would have gone as well as *Nabucco* and *I Lombardi* did in Milan. Guasco [the tenor] had no voice at all, and was so hoarse it was frightening. It is impossible to sing more out of tune than la Loewe did last night. Every number, big or small, was applauded, with the exception of Guasco's cavatina; but the most effective pieces of all were Loewe's cabaletta, the cabaletta of a duet that ends as a trio, the whole of the first act finale, the whole of the conspiracy act, and the trio of the fourth act. They took three curtain calls after the first act, one after the second, three after the third, and three or four at the end of the opera. That's the true story.

26

Piave, collaborating with Verdi for the first time on *Ernani*, was to become the composer's favourite librettist until the magnificent partnership with Boito which began years after Piave's death and which produced *Otello* and *Falstaff*. For his next seventeen operas after *Ernani*, Verdi's choice of librettist was usually made between Piave, Solera and Salvatore Cammarano. Piave was responsible for the libretti of nine of Verdi's twenty-six operas, followed by Solera and Cammarano with four each, and Boito with two. No other librettist collaborated with Verdi more than once. He was a hard task-master, and since he himself had a very clearly defined idea of what he wanted a libretto to be and was perfectly capable of drafting it in outline himself, what he needed was not so much a skilful librettist as a superior literary secretary. No doubt Verdi favoured Piave because he did as he was told. His letters to Piave clearly indicate the nature of their professional relationship. 'I have received your verses and I don't like them. You talk to me about 100 syllables!! And it's obvious that 100 syllables aren't enough when you take 25 to say the sun is setting!!!' That sentence comes from their correspondence concerning a revision of *La forza del destino*, after they had been working together for more than twenty years. But it would be wrong to think of Piave as nothing more than a good-natured hack. Verdi certainly thought more highly of him, and more than once defended him against unfair criticism. 'A libretto that bears Piave's name', he wrote to a friend shortly after the première of *Simon Boccanegra* in 1857, 'is judged in advance as the worst possible poetry, but, frankly, I know I would be content if I could write verses as good as "Vieni a mirar la cerula … Delle faci festanti al barlume".'

Piave was by no means the least good poet among Verdi's librettists. His compression of Victor Hugo's play into the opera *Ernani* is expertly done, and even if one gives the composer the credit

Francesco Maria Piave, who was probably Verdi's favourite librettist.

for selecting the scenes to be adapted and for reshaping the plot, Piave deserves nothing but praise for his verse, which is simple, direct and immensely singable. Not infrequently the Italian verse is a direct translation of Hugo, though there is much that is completely original. The opera itself marks a significant advance in Verdi's dramatic style, and in his musical characterization. Melodically, it is even richer than *Nabucco* and *I Lombardi*, and its weak passages are fewer. Some of Verdi's uniquely individual effects occur throughout the opera: the wide, arching phrases for soprano, the warm cantilena, the glorious tunes written high in the baritone's range, the compassionate orchestral comment, and the irresistible onward motion of the ensembles. The ensemble in the third act finale includes the famous cry 'A Carlo Quinto sia gloria ed onor' (Glory and honour to Charles V) sung to an emotionally affecting phrase which was picked out by Roman audiences three years after the first Venice performances, and turned into a tribute to the newly elected Pope Pius IX, of whom the liberals had great hopes. '*A Pio Nono*', 'To Pius IX be glory and honour', they sang.

The theme played on the horn by Silva in the last scene of *Ernani*, a theme heard first at the beginning of the orchestral prelude to the opera, is Verdi's earliest use of a form of *Leitmotiv* (or leading motive). Since he has often been accused of appropriating the *Leitmotiv* from Wagner, it is worth mentioning that, in 1844, no Wagner operas had been staged in Italy, nor had Verdi seen any Wagner scores. *Der fliegende Holländer*, which had been performed in Germany the previous year, had not been published.

Verdi had a tendency to underestimate his successful first nights and exaggerate his failures. The 'pleasant enough success' of *Ernani* developed at subsequent performances, as the singers improved and audiences became more and more enthusiastic. Only two months after the Fenice season ended, the opera was staged at another Venetian theatre, the Teatro San Benedetto, this time with enormous success.

Verdi himself had left Venice after fulfilling his obligations by conducting the first three performances at the Fenice. He had not been especially pleased with his singers, and he was not particularly fond of Venice. Soon after his arrival there to rehearse *I Lombardi* and compose *Ernani*, he had written to a friend: 'Venice is beautiful, it's poetic, it's divine, but I wouldn't stay here voluntarily... Laugh if you like, but I shall be back in Milan as soon as *Ernani* gets on to the stage.' And he was. At the age of thirty he was now eagerly sought after by both impresarios and society hostesses. The latter he avoided as much as possible, while for the former he began to work assiduously, producing ten new operas in the next six years.

Above: Playbill for the first performance of Ernani, *at the Teatro la Fenice, Venice.*
Right: Sketch by Abd' Elkader Farrah for the Sadler's Wells Theatre production of Ernani, *1967.*

Verdi was now so busy that his old friend and benefactor Antonio Barezzi realized that he must have a musical secretary or assistant of some kind. And so Barezzi arranged for a twenty-two-year-old music student, a poor youth from a village near Busseto just as Verdi had once been, to come to Milan and have lessons with Verdi in return for acting as his amanuensis. The naïve young Emanuele Muzio loved and idolized his gruff but good-natured teacher, and Verdi in turn became strongly attached to Muzio.

Back in Milan after *Ernani*, Verdi considered offers from several Italian theatres, among them La Scala, the Fenice and the Teatro San Carlo, Naples; he finally accepted an offer from the Teatro Argentina in Rome to write a new opera for performance in the autumn of 1844. As it was already spring, there was not a great deal of time in which to choose a subject and prepare a libretto. Verdi's first suggestion was for an opera on Lorenzino de' Medici, but this proved unacceptable to the papal censors. His second suggestion, which was approved, was Byron's play *The Two Foscari*, and, since he and Piave had already considered it in Venice the previous year before deciding upon *Ernani*, Piave was entrusted with the task of writing a libretto, under the strict supervision of the composer, who wrote to him in May:

> ...think carefully and try to continue as you have begun. So far everything is going beautifully, except for one small thing. I notice that, up to here, nothing has been said about the crime for which Foscari is sentenced. It seems to me that should be emphasized.
>
> In the tenor's cavatina, there are two things which don't work well: the first is that, having finished his cavatina, Jacopo remains on the stage, and this always weakens the effect. Second, there is no contrasting idea to set against the adagio. So write a little bit of dialogue between the soldier and Jacopo, and then have an officer say 'Bring in the prisoner'. Follow this with a cabaletta; but make it a strong

Verdi's benefactor, father-in-law and friend, Antonio Barezzi.

one for we are writing for Rome. And then, as I say, the character of Foscari must be made more energetic. The woman's cavatina is excellent. I think that here you should insert a very short recitative, then a solo passage for the Doge and a big duet. This duet, coming at the end, should be quite short. Work yourself into a proper state of feeling and write some beautiful verses. In the second act, write a romanza for Jacopo, and don't forget the duet with Maria [whose name was changed in the opera to Lucrezia], then the great trio, followed by the chorus and finale. In the third act, do just as we agreed, and try to make the gondolier's song blend with a chorus of citizens. Could it not be arranged for this to happen towards evening, so that we could have a sunset too, which would be beautiful?

During the composition of *I due Foscari*, Verdi became afflicted with headaches, stomach pains, and a continually sore throat, psychosomatic illnesses which were to attend his creative processes for the remainder of his life. But by the end of September the opera was virtually complete, and Verdi left Milan for Rome where he spent the month of October orchestrating his work and rehearsing it. On 3 November he conducted the first performance, which was well received, although the audience expressed some annoyance with the management, who had raised the ticket prices. However, the second and third performances, at regular prices though also conducted by Verdi, were greeted with immense enthusiasm. On the second night the composer took thirty curtain-calls.

There is in *I due Foscari* less of the almost brutal energy that animates *Nabucco* and *I Lombardi*, and more of the melancholy which was a strong element in Verdi's temperament. What is most remarkable about the opera is its atmosphere, and the way in which this is created in the orchestra. Verdi gives more prominence to woodwind instruments than in his earlier operas, from the solo clarinet and flute writing in the Overture to the clarinet and bassoon colours which contribute to the shadowy gloom which predominates

Teatro Argentina, Rome, where I due Foscari *was first performed.*

throughout the opera. Although he subscribed to the general view that the Italian musical genius was for vocal music, as opposed to the Germans who excelled in the symphony and the string quartet, Verdi was always much more aware than his immediate predecessors of the importance of the orchestra in opera. As early as *Nabucco* he had begun to experiment with his instrumentation, and *I due Foscari* marks an important step forward. Nowhere in the opera does the darkly pessimistic orchestral colour seem merely applied to the vocal line: it is always used as an intrinsic element in the sound texture. Verdi once told a correspondent: 'The idea comes to me all of a piece, and I hear immediately whether a certain note ought to be played by flute or violin. The difficulty lies in getting it down on paper quickly enough and in attempting to express the musical idea exactly as it enters my mind.' In *I due Foscari* Verdi almost completely succeeded in setting down as an integrated whole the vision of gloom and *accidia* which Byron's play suggested to him. It is one of the most individual of his pre-*Rigoletto* operas, compact of shape, sensitively scored and full of that heartfelt, apparently spontaneous melody to which only he and Schubert had unlimited access.

At the end of November, Verdi returned to Milan where he was due to produce a revival of *I Lombardi* at La Scala and also to compose a new work for that theatre where his first four operas had been staged. But he found that standards at La

Scala had declined since he had last worked there. The arrangement of the orchestra was unsatisfactory, the singers took liberties with his music, the chorus was lazy and ill-disciplined, and the scenic department had been allowed to run down. Young Muzio wrote to Barezzi to say that, at rehearsals, Verdi was continually shouting 'like a madman' and stamping his feet. Despite, or perhaps because of, all this, the revival of *I Lombardi* on 26 December 1844 was successful, and Verdi was now able to devote his full attention to the new opera which he had already begun to compose. The subject chosen was Joan of Arc, and Temistocle Solera, who had written the libretti of *Nabucco* and *I Lombardi*, set to work to concoct a libretto based on Schiller's play, *Die Jungfrau von Orleans*.

Writing to Barezzi in Busseto, Muzio described the music enthusiastically and uncritically as it came from Verdi's pen. According to him the 'terrifying introduction' to *Giovanna d'Arco* was inspired by the rocky precipices of the Apennine passes through which the composer had travelled on his way back to Milan from Rome. 'The demons' choruses', Muzio continued, 'are original, popular, truly Italian. The first, "Tu sei bella", is a most graceful waltz, full of seductive motifs that, after only two hearings, can be sung straightaway. The second, "Vittoria, Vittoria, s'applauda a Satana", is music of diabolical exaltation, music that makes one shudder and tremble.' Of the love duet for Giovanna and Carlo, he wrote: 'This is the grandest and most magnificent piece in the opera.'

The opera was written in less than eight weeks, and was given its first performance at La Scala on 15 February 1845. It proved extremely popular with audiences though less so with critics, and was given four performances a week until the end of the season. Within three months it had been produced in Rome, and during the following decade there were productions in Madrid, Lisbon, St Petersburg, Malta, Buenos Aires and Santiago, Chile. In some Italian towns, religious objections

to the subject necessitated the music being fitted to a new libretto with the title *Orietta di Lesbo*!

Solera claimed that his libretto was a completely original piece of work, but an examination of it makes it clear that his source was Schiller's play. His *Giovanna d'Arco* has been described as the epitome of the really absurd opera libretto, and the fact that it is an adaptation of Schiller has been used to imply that a certain degree of desecration or travesty has been indulged in as well. Although it is true that Solera's Giovanna has practically no point of contact with the historical Jeanne d'Arc, it should be remembered that this is equally true of Schiller's *Jungfrau von Orleans*. Written in 1801 while Voltaire's satirical poem on Joan, *La Pucelle*, was still being widely read, Schiller's play made no pretence to historical accuracy. In his correspondence with Goethe, Schiller had expressed the belief that art could best flourish by avoiding the strict imitation of nature. Instead, he advocated introducing symbolic aids to take the place of the object represented. Such symbolism, which Schiller believed would purify theatrical art, raising it to the level of poetry, was employed in *Die Jungfrau von Orleans*: his interest was not in historical reality but in poetic truth, and to him the inner symbolic truth of Joan of Arc rendered her death at the stake unnecessary. In an essay on Schiller, Thomas Mann referred to *Die Jungfrau* as a 'word-opera'. Verdi had already intuitively realized this, but his mistake lay in imagining that the play's poetic identity could survive the inevitable compression required by adaptation to the lyric stage. Solera not only cut several scenes, he also made significant alterations, the most damaging of which is his having Joan fall in love with the French Dauphin instead of, as in Schiller, the handsome young Englishman, Lionel. In Schiller's play Joan's dilemma is brought about by the opposing claims of her mission and her love. Solera's change reduces the action to a completely personal level, the protagonists being Joan, her father and the Dauphin. It was understandable that the romantic Schiller, like Byron and Hugo, should appeal both to Verdi's temperament and to his political liberalism, but it was a pity that Solera failed to understand the poet's intentions, and that Verdi seems, unusually for him, not to have exercised any control over his librettist.

Giovanna d'Arco, then, has its dramatic short-comings, but musically it is one of the most attractive of Verdi's early operas. In orchestral colouring and in vocal character it is completely different from its immediate predecessor, *I due Foscari*. The Overture, a sinfonia in three sections, is particularly interesting; its central *andante*, pastorally scored for solo flute, clarinet and oboe, and

Below: Temistocle Solera, who wrote the libretti for Nabucco *and three other Verdi operas.*
Right: Playbill for a production of Giovanna d'Arco *at the Teatro San Carlo, Naples, in 1951.*

CITTÀ DI NAPOLI
TEATRO DI S. CARLO
CELEBRAZIONI VERDIANE
Giovanna D'Arco
CON
GINO PENNO
RENATA TEBALDI
UGO SAVARESE
REGIA DI
E. FRIGERIO
MAESTRO DIRETTORE E CONCERTATORE
GABRIELE SANTINI
ALLESTIMENTO DI
C.M. CRISTINI
PRIMA RAPPRESENTAZIONE 15 MARZO 1951

presumably intended to suggest Giovanna's life before her voices began calling her, is quite beautiful. The theme of the Overture's final *allegro* is virtually identical with the broad central tune in the Overture to *Les Vêpres siciliennes*, composed ten years later. They are basically the same tune, the only important difference being one of tempo. This is unusual, for Verdi was not given to conscious self-borrowing as was Rossini or Donizetti.

The opera is divided into a Prologue and three acts. In the opening scene of the Prologue, the chorus in which the citizens tell of their horror of the haunted spot is a by no means unworthy forerunner of the storm music in *Otello*, while the scene in the haunted forest itself opens with a marvellously eerie orchestral introduction which would not seem out of place in *Der Freischütz*. The arioso-like recitative for Giovanna's father, Giacomo, in this scene is eloquent and urgent; two or three years earlier Verdi would have followed it with a cavatina, but he is now experienced enough, and confident enough, to do no such thing. He has nothing against the accepted forms; indeed, as late as *Aida* he will ask his librettist to allow for cabalettas; but he is ready now to sacrifice form to the requirements of the drama.

Giovanna's cavatina, 'Sempre all' alba', is one of those early manifestations of Verdi's genius which occur somewhere in every score he wrote. Its accompaniment is translucent, its vocal figuration delicate yet strong. When it is finished, Giovanna does not launch into a cabaletta: she sings a few bars of arioso and goes to sleep. The chorus of demons who visit her in sleep are not at all frightening, *pace* Muzio. Verdi was doubtless aiming at something like the seductive and dangerous sweetness of the Erlking's utterances in Schubert's song, but his demons in 3/8 time remain disarmingly jolly. The chorus of angels, curiously, is somewhat more Schubertian.

The score of *Giovanna d'Arco* contains considerably more felicities than miscalculations. In Act I, Giovanna's aria 'O fatidica foresta' is like a water-colour sketch for the oil painting of Aida's 'O patria mia'. Later, when Giovanna hears the demons mocking her while Carlo continues to sing of his love for her, the effect is tremendous, out of all proportion to the absurd yet touching means employed. In the triumphal march which opens Act II, Verdi makes splendid use of his much-favoured device of the stage band. The broad tune of the march is quite indefensible against the charge of banality, but it can reduce to tears anyone who deeply responds to Verdi. Others will recognize it only as the ancestor of a certain chorus in *The Pirates of Penzance*. The Act III finale is made memorable by the sheer flourish of Giovanna's gloriously drawn phrase, 'Addio terra, addio gloria mortale'. It occurs only once: Verdi was too prolific a melodist to 'plug' his best tunes.

Not all of *Giovanna d'Arco* is on the level of its finest numbers, but, in addition to the melodic generosity and youthful resilience which it shares with the other operas of Verdi's 'galley years', it possesses a curiously primitive but pervasive charm of its own. No excuses need be made for it.

Immediately after the first performance of *Giovanna d'Arco*, Merelli asked Verdi to direct a production of *Ernani* at La Scala. Verdi not only declined, he also publicly stated that he would have nothing further to do with La Scala because of his profound dissatisfaction with the management of the theatre. This seems ungracious and indeed ungrateful behaviour on Verdi's part, for Merelli, had, after all, staged his first operas and had demonstrated his faith in the young Verdi before it was by any means assured that he would make his way to the forefront of Italian composers. It is true that Verdi was, in some respects, a harsh man, but he was also scrupulously just in his dealings with others, and he expected to be treated fairly in return. He now felt bitter towards Merelli and La Scala for, as he considered, not taking enough care over the staging of his operas. The fact that, some months later, Merelli put on *I due Foscari* without Verdi's collaboration and with the second and third acts in reverse order did nothing to ease the situation. Verdi was determined in future not to allow his operas to have their premières at La Scala. Nearly a quarter of a century was to pass before he relented and allowed the revised version of *La forza del destino*, seen first in its original version in St Petersburg, to be staged there. But the next real world première of a Verdi opera at La Scala after 1845 was not until *Otello* in 1887. Between these years Verdi's operas, among them several of his greatest masterpieces, received their initial performances in Naples, Venice, Florence, London, Paris, Trieste, Rome, St Petersburg and Cairo. The leading Italian opera house was boycotted by the leading Italian composer.

After *Giovanna d'Arco*, Verdi's next commission was from the management of the Teatro San Carlo in Naples, for whom he had already agreed

Teatro San Carlo, Naples, where Verdi's Alzira *was first performed in 1845.*

to write an opera for performance in June 1845, a mere four months after the première of *Giovanna*. The subject, Voltaire's play *Alzire*, had been chosen the previous year, and the Neapolitan librettist Salvatore Cammarano, who had already achieved a certain fame for his work with Donizetti and other composers (he had written the libretto of *Lucia di Lammermoor* ten years earlier), had been engaged to collaborate with Verdi. 'I am accused of liking a great deal of noise and handling the singing badly', the composer had written to Cammarano. 'Pay no attention to this. Just put passion into it, and you will see that I write reasonably well.'

The date of the first performance of *Alzira* had to be altered, for Verdi's usual nervous headaches, sore throats and stomach pains returned during composition of the new work. Verdi was as often as not late in delivering his operas, but never very late. This time he asked for a postponement of two months, which was granted by the Naples

impresario Vincenzo Flauto only with the greatest reluctance. Flauto was not disposed to take Verdi's illness too seriously, and, when he lightly suggested Verdi's health would be sure to improve as soon as he came down to sunny Naples and started work, Verdi's response was characteristically irritable. To Flauto, he wrote: 'I am terribly sorry to have to inform you that my illness is not as minor as you think it is, and the absinthe tincture will be of no use to me. You say that the stimulating air of Vesuvius will improve my health, but I can assure you that what I need to get well again is calm and rest.' To Cammarano he complained of the style of Flauto's letter, expressed annoyance that the medical certificate he had sent to Flauto should be viewed with scepticism, and added: 'If it were not for the pleasure of setting your libretto to music, and writing for that theatre, I should have followed the advice of the doctor who advised me to rest all summer.'

An illness is no less serious, pains are no less painful, simply because they may be psychosomatically induced. Verdi's physical symptoms, it became obvious the following year, were also masking a deep psychological unrest. But, in the spring of 1845, he continued to write to librettist and impresario about his illness with as much energy as might have sufficed to produce the opera. 'We artists are never allowed to be ill. We should not always bother to behave like gentlemen, for the impresarios please themselves as to whether they believe us or not.' This to Cammarano, and to Flauto: 'You tell me I am under an obligation to the administration. But if even sick prisoners are shown consideration, why shouldn't I be?'

Finally, however, Verdi arrived in Naples, completed his opera and rehearsed it; *Alzira* had its first performance at the Teatro San Carlo on 12 August 1845. Its success was no more than moderate, and it was received stonily some months later in Rome, and the following February in Parma. After the Rome performances Verdi confessed to a friend that the flaws in 'poor, unfortunate *Alzira*'

were too deeply rooted for him to improve the opera by revision, and years later he is reported to have said of it: 'Quella è proprio brutta' (That one's really bad). After productions in Lisbon and Barcelona in 1849, and Malta in 1858, *Alzira* appears not to have been revived again until a broadcast from Vienna in 1936 and a stage production in Rome in 1967. It vies with *Il corsaro*, which he composed three years later, for the distinction of being Verdi's least successful opera.

Alzira's lack of success can hardly be denied, but perhaps it can be defended from the unfavourable judgement of critics who have examined it in vocal score but have never seen it staged, and even from the denigration apparently uttered by its own composer. There is little that can be said in favour of Cammarano's libretto other than it follows the events of Voltaire's *Alzire* reasonably closely. Voltaire's play about the unfortunate encounter of the sixteenth-century Incas with Christian morality may or may not have been written with atheistic tongue in cheek: the point is academic when one comes to consider its compression by Cammarano into a rather brutal adventure story. It is not easy to understand the attraction of the subject for Verdi, whose liberal agnosticism was allied with a deeply ingrained anti-clericalism which led to his detesting all talk of religion. He would have been interested neither in proving the Christian God morally superior to the Inca gods nor in ironically implying the contrary. It may have been the exotic locale which appealed to him, though he made no attempt to write Indian music for *Alzira* comparable to his invented Egyptian music for *Aida* twenty-six years later. Instead he clothed Cammarano's terse poetry in music of vigorous rhythm and attractive melody. Although in earlier operas he had quite frequently forsaken the old formula of introductory chorus, recitative, cavatina, recitative, cabaletta, in *Alzira* Verdi accepted the conventional

Virginia Zeani and Gianfranco Cecchele in Alzira *at the Teatro dell' Opera, Rome, in 1967.*

formal structure of Cammarano's libretto without question. As a result the opera (to which, perhaps because of his illness, he appears not to have been deeply committed) is finally unsatisfactory and dramatically naïve, though it contains much excellent and beautiful music, and can generate a certain theatrical excitement in performance.

Returning to Milan in August 1845, Verdi turned his attention to an opera which he had agreed to compose for the Teatro la Fenice in Venice, where *Ernani* had had its successful première the previous year. He had become interested in a play about Attila the Hun, by a minor German dramatist, Zacharias Werner, and had already sent a copy of the play to Francesco Piave, his Venice librettist. But he now decided that the gentle Piave was not the right person for this particular job, and instead entrusted the libretto of *Attila* to Temistocle Solera whom he had last worked with on *Giovanna d'Arco*. While the lazy and unreliable Solera was intermittently at work on the libretto, Verdi tried to concentrate on his other business affairs, offers from London and Paris and from various publishers, and kept his hand in by composing six songs to texts by several poets. These were published not by the firm of Ricordi but by one of Ricordi's rivals, Francesco Lucca, for whom Verdi had also agreed to write an opera. He had, however, taken on too many commitments and, finding himself harassed by managements, agents and publishers, he reacted by sinking into neurotic lethargy. He left Milan to spend a few weeks in Busseto, but found it impossible to work there, and soon returned in a state of nervous instability and pessimistic gloom. 'Thanks for the news of *Alzira*', he wrote to a correspondent in November,

> but more for remembering your poor friend, condemned continually to scribble musical

Left: Gaetano Fraschini (tenor), who sang Zamoro in the first production of Alzira.
Right: Francesco Lucca, the publisher for whom Verdi wrote Il corsaro.

41

notes. God save the ears of every good Christian from having to listen to them! Accursed notes! How am I, physically and spiritually? Physically I am well, but my mind is black, always black, and will be so until I have finished with this career which I abhor. And afterwards? It's useless to delude oneself. It will always be black. Happiness doesn't exist for me.

Emanuele Muzio eventually extracted the *Attila* libretto from Solera after a series of unsuccessful visits ('that lazy dog of a poet hasn't done a thing...this morning at eleven o'clock he was still in bed'), and Verdi began to compose the opera. But he was interrupted by a severe attack of rheumatism and was forced to take to his bed and submit to being massaged frequently by the faithful Muzio. When he arrived in Venice in December to produce *Attila*, he had written hardly any of it. Certain alterations to the final act of the libretto were necessary, and, as Solera had gone to Spain, Piave made some changes and wrote the additional verses required. The opening night was postponed and Verdi continued to work on the opera, but early in January he succumbed to a severe form of gastric fever and was confined to bed for three weeks. Meanwhile, *Giovanna d'Arco* had been produced at the Fenice, in the presence of the Tsar of Russia. Verdi, having written a new aria for the Fenice's Giovanna, Sophie Loewe, was too ill to attend the performance. Work on *Attila* progressed slowly, interrupted by a return of the gastric fever. Verdi eventually finished the opera while still in bed, in what he exaggeratedly referred to as 'an almost dying condition'.

When, at long last, *Attila* reached the stage on 17 March 1846, eleven weeks late, it was an enormous success. The Venetian audience was understandably affected by the scene in which refugees from the sacked town of Aquileia arrive at the lagoon to found the city of Venice, and they proved themselves as sensitive as the Milanese to the political implications of battle between Italians and Huns. When the Roman general Ezio, in a duet with Attila, sang the line 'Avrai tu l'universo, resti l'Italia a me' (Take the universe, but leave me Italy), there were shouts from the packed theatre of 'A noi! A noi! L'Italia a noi!' The shouters appear not to have realized that, in the year A.D. 54, 'l'universo' would be taken to mean the Italian peninsula and 'l'Italia' to mean Rome. Also, Ezio's meaning is not 'leave us in peace', but 'I'll help you to the rest if you allow me to take over Rome'.

After the first performance of *Attila*, Verdi found himself fêted as a hero by the Venetians, and escorted to his hotel 'with flowers, bands and torches'. To his friend the Countess Maffei he wrote: '*Attila* had a fair enough success. The applause and the calls were too much for a poor sick man. Perhaps it was not completely understood, though it may be this evening. My friends would say that this is the best of my operas. The public questions that. I say it is not inferior to any of the others. Time will tell.'

The original play, *Attila, König der Hunnen* by Werner, is a more complex work of art than Verdi's opera, despite the turgidity of its sentiment and the occasional clumsiness of its language. Werner was writing a dramatic essay on the concept of fate, which Verdi and Solera turned into an opera about patriotism. Indeed, so convinced were they of the rectitude of the Italian cause that they appear not to have noticed that, in their opera, the Italians behave treacherously while Attila the Hun displays a certain magnanimity. If, nevertheless, the opera succeeds on its own level, it is due to the forcefulness of Verdi's writing for the voices and the ever-increasing skill and imagination he exhibits in his use of the orchestra. But his own estimate of *Attila* as not inferior to any of the earlier operas is surely open to question. His musical characterization is temporarily at a standstill, and the presence in his score of a few fine arias and one beautiful trio ('Te sol quest' anima') is not sufficient to raise the merely acceptable *Attila* to the level of the really exciting *Nabucco* or *Ernani*.

3 The 'Galley Years' II: Macbeth **to** Stiffelio

Verdi's friend Andrea Maffei, husband of the Countess Clarina Maffei, had attended the première of *Attila* in Venice, and he accompanied the ailing composer back to Milan. Verdi was now expected in London, where he had agreed to write for the impresario Benjamin Lumley an opera which might well have turned out to be *King Lear*. But he was too ill to travel, and his doctors insisted that instead he take six months' complete rest. So for six months Verdi was cared for devotedly by Muzio, according to whom he did nothing in the way of writing or study, but amused himself 'with walks, or drives in one of the five or six carriages at his disposal'. In July, accompanied

Andrea Maffei, Verdi's friend and the librettist of I masnadieri.

by Andrea Maffei, he took the waters at the tiny spa of Recoaro in the foothills of the Venetian Alps, but he soon became bored by the sun, the fresh mountain air, the baths and healthy walks, and by the end of the month was back in Milan.

Verdi was now being pressed by both Benjamin Lumley and the publisher Francesco Lucca for whom he had also agreed to write an opera. In addition, the Paris Opéra wanted him to write for them, and Alessandro Lanari, impresario of the Teatro della Pergola in Florence, where *Attila* had been performed with enormous success, persuaded Verdi to agree to compose a new opera for his theatre. Flauto, from Naples, reminded the composer that he had promised to write a new opera for the Teatro San Carlo in 1847. While he had been convalescing in Recoaro. Verdi had turned over in his mind several ideas for operas. He did a considerable amount of work planning a libretto on *Die Ahnfrau*, a play by the Austrian poet and playwright Grillparzer, but nothing was to come of it. Schiller's play *Die Räuber* eventually became Verdi's choice for his London opera, which he postponed for one year. He decided first to compose the opera for Florence, and for a time wavered between *Die Räuber* and Shakespeare's *Macbeth*. The final choice of *Macbeth* for Florence was determined by the availability of appropriate singers. The tenor whom Verdi wanted for the Schiller opera was under contract elsewhere, and *Macbeth* did not require a leading tenor as Verdi intended to write the title role for baritone. *Macbeth* was sent to Piave to be turned into Italian verse, but only after Verdi had chosen the scenes to be included and written the entire libretto himself in Italian prose. By October Verdi had begun to compose the music. As though he

Above: Cover of the vocal score of Macbeth.
Right: Marianna Barbieri-Nini (soprano), who sang Lady Macbeth in the first production.

realized this was the most important task he had taken on so far, he worked slowly, for three or four hours most mornings, and sometimes in the evening as well. By January 1847 the opera was completely sketched out and he had begun to orchestrate. In mid-February he arrived in Florence with a finished score ready to rehearse. He had taken immense pains to ensure that the opera was produced along the correct Shakespearean lines. In a letter to the impresario Alessandro Lanari he had given precise instructions regarding the appearance of Banquo's ghost, adding: 'I found all this out from London where they have been performing this tragedy continually for more than two hundred years.' The scene designer was informed that he was mistaken about the period, and was given a potted lesson in British history:

'... the era in which Macbeth takes place is much later than Ossian and the Roman Empire. Macbeth assassinated Duncan in 1040, and he himself was killed in 1057. In 1039 England was ruled by Harold, called Harefoot, out of Danish extraction. He was succeeded in the same year by Hardicanute, half-brother of Edward the Confessor.'

There is no doubt that Verdi felt strongly committed to his first opera on a play by his beloved Shakespeare. In dedicating the score to Antonio Barezzi, he wrote:

Dear father-in-law,
For a long time I have wanted to dedicate an

opera to you who have been father, benefactor and friend to me. It is a duty I should have performed sooner, and would have if circumstances had not prevented me. Here now is this *Macbeth*, which is dearer to me than all my other operas, and which I therefore deem more worthy of being presented to you. It comes from my heart: let yours receive it, and let it always bear testimony to the gratitude and affection felt for you by

Your most affectionate
G. Verdi.

Verdi was accompanied to Florence by Muzio, who was to play for the piano rehearsals. The singers soon found themselves working much harder than was usual for them. Verdi made a point of telling the Macbeth, Felice Varesi (who was later to be the first Rigoletto, and the first Germont in *La traviata*), to attempt to interpret the poet first, not the composer. The singer of Lady Macbeth, Marianna Barbieri-Nini, wrote an account of the rehearsal period in which she describes the composer rehearsing the duet in Act I:

The evening of the final rehearsal, with the theatre full of guests, Verdi made the artists put on their costumes, and when he insisted on something woe betide those who contradicted him. When we were dressed and ready, with the orchestra in the pit and the chorus already on stage, Verdi beckoned to me and Varesi to follow him into the wings. We did so, and he explained that he wanted us to come out into the foyer for another piano rehearsal of that wretched duet.

'Maestro,' I protested, 'we are already in our Scottish costumes. How can we?'

'Put cloaks over them.'

Varesi, annoyed at this strange request, dared to raise his voice: 'But, for God's sake, we've already rehearsed it a hundred and fifty times.'

'I wouldn't say that if I were you, for within half an hour it will be a hundred and fifty-one.'

He was a tyrant whom one had to obey. I can still remember the black look Varesi threw at Verdi as he followed the Maestro into the foyer. With his hand clutching the hilt of his sword he looked as though he would murder Verdi just as later he would murder Duncan. But even

Varesi gave in, and the one hundred and fifty-first rehearsal took place, while inside the theatre the audience waited impatiently.

The opera was given a highly successful first performance at the Teatro della Pergola on 14 March 1847. The Florentine audience called Verdi on stage thirty-eight times, and the following performances were equally well received. Later in the year *Macbeth* began to be produced at other Italian theatres. Eighteen years later, in 1865, Verdi made some revisions for the first Paris production, at the same time adding the ballet music which was almost statutory for Paris. But the opera as we know it today is still basically the work of the thirty-four-year-old Verdi of 1847. The alterations and additions of middle age are not particularly significant: it is good to have Lady Macbeth's splendid aria 'La luce langue', but it is worth remembering that all the other great moments in the opera were there from the beginning. With *Macbeth*, Verdi ceased being a purveyor of popular entertainment, as Rossini and Donizetti had been forced to be by the operatic conditions prevailing in their day, and began to be a serious artist.

To say that, of course, is to over-simplify the situation. The composer of *Il barbiere di Siviglia* was a serious artist, and so was the composer of *Lucia di Lammermoor*. But both men spent almost their entire professional lives working against time, and neither of them concerned himself much with opera as drama. Verdi was a real musical dramatist, in a sense in which the term could never be applied to Rossini or Donizetti, and from *Macbeth* onwards he was to occupy himself increasingly with the staging of his operas, with only one exception: *Il corsaro* in the following year, 1848. An interesting letter, written by Verdi in 1848 to Salvatore Cammarano who was producing *Macbeth* in Naples, reveals the importance he ascribed to the actual timbre of Lady Macbeth's voice. The Naples Lady Macbeth was to be Eugenia Tadolini, a soprano whom Verdi admired and who had created the title role in *Alzira* three years earlier.

Teatro della Pergola, Florence, where Macbeth *was first performed in 1847.*

But Tadolini, Verdi claimed, was too fine a singer for Lady Macbeth.

This may seem to you absurd, but Tadolini has a beautiful and attractive figure, and I want Lady Macbeth to be ugly and evil. Tadolini sings to perfection, and I don't want Lady Macbeth to sing at all. Tadolini has a wonderful voice, clear, flexible, strong, while Lady Macbeth's voice should be hard, stifled and dark. Tadolini's voice is angelic; I want Lady Macbeth's to be diabolic.

Throughout *Macbeth*, Verdi was concerned to stress the dramatic values. The old formulas are discarded, and the music is free to respond directly and immediately to the requirements of the drama. From the terse, Beethovenian Prelude to the final chorus of victory, everything in the opera underlines and emphasizes the drama. Above the opening bars of the witches' chorus at the beginning of Act I, Verdi wrote: 'Nè dimenticarsi che sono streghe che parlano' (Don't forget it's witches who are talking). The old musical forms have become extremely fluid. The scene of Banquo and Macbeth in their first confrontation with the witches does not consist of chorus, recitative, *andante*, chorus, cabaletta. Macbeth and Banquo exchange only a few bars of recitative after the witches vanish, and Macbeth's reaction to the male chorus's information that Duncan has made him Thane of Cawdor is expressed in a poignantly uneasy *andante* that lies somewhere between arioso and aria. Even in more conventional passages, such as Lady Macbeth's aria and cabaletta

in the second scene of Act I, Verdi manages to parallel Shakespeare closely. It is, in fact, when he takes a bold, imaginative leap, trusting in his own genius, that he lands nearest to Shakespeare.

The music accompanying the procession of Duncan and his retinue into Macbeth's castle is frequently cut severely by conductors who have been persuaded it is banal and provincial. But it is significant that Verdi did not, in the course of his 1865 revision of the opera, attempt to alter it. The apparent banality of this music for the stage band is perhaps the earliest instance of what we know today as Brechtian *Verfremdungseffekt*, or distancing effect. Verdi did not want Duncan to intrude into the drama: for him, *Macbeth* is not a story of the murder of a kindly old king, it is

an exploration of the psyches of Macbeth and Lady Macbeth. He omits Duncan's earlier two scenes, and robs him of speech in his remaining scene. Soon to be despatched to another world, Duncan already exists in another sound-world. Verdi's tune is eerie, but significant in the same way that Mahler's sudden intrusion of a simple hurdy-gurdy tune into a complex symphonic argument is significant. That Verdi was capable of using music to express dramatic irony is borne out by his remarkable banqueting scene in Act II.

To claim that *Macbeth* is the earliest of Verdi's masterpieces is not to denigrate the impressive achievement of several earlier operas. But in *Macbeth* Verdi made a huge advance towards dramatic truth, without sacrificing any part of his unique melodic gift. Though the operas between *Macbeth* and *Rigoletto* were to include one or two of his less impressive creations, Verdi had, with *Macbeth*, revealed the heights to which he could rise.

Previous page: The final scene from a Glyndebourne production of Macbeth, *with (inset) Kostas Paskalis (baritone) as Macbeth.*
Below: Costume designs by Carol Lawrence for the Welsh National Opera production of I masnadieri.
Right: Luigi Lablache (bass), who sang Count Moor in the first production of I masnadieri.

With *Macbeth* behind him, Verdi was now free to turn his attention to the opera he was committed to write for London, *I masnadieri*, based on Schiller's play *Die Räuber*. He had already considered *King Lear* as a possible subject for London, though he had rejected it for Venice three years earlier. In fact, terms had been agreed between Verdi and the English impresario Benjamin Lumley for the composition of *King Lear*, on the understanding that the role of Lear would be written for the great French–Irish bass Luigi Lablache, who was then in his early fifties. It was Verdi's illness in 1846 which led to the postponement of the London project until the following year. Lumley's star attraction was now Jenny Lind, the 'Swedish nightingale', around whom

Verdi planned *I masnadieri*. Lablache was in Lumley's company, but was given the comparatively minor role of Count Moor. Throughout his entire life, Verdi was to continue to be attracted by the idea of composing *Lear*, and then to shy away from it at the last moment. There were always perfectly feasible practical reasons for his doing so, but there must surely have been some deeper psychological reason why he failed to attempt something he so clearly wanted to do. When Verdi was eighty-three, the young Mascagni asked him why he had never written the opera. 'Verdi closed his eyes for a moment, perhaps to

Interior of Her Majesty's Theatre, London, as it was in 1847 when I masnadieri *was produced there.*

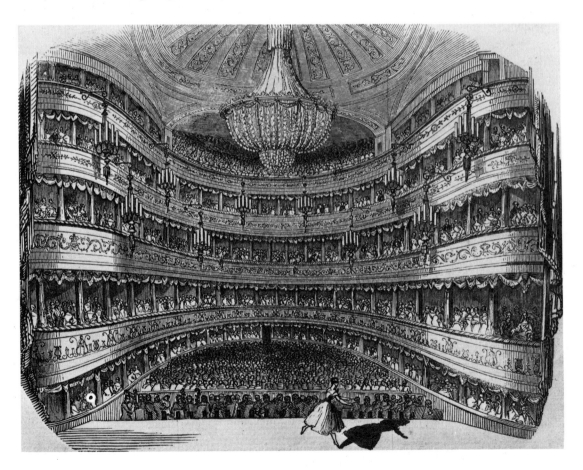

remember, perhaps to forget. Then softly and slowly he replied: ' "The scene in which King Lear finds himself on the heath terrified me." ' Perhaps he was troubled by Shakespeare's realistic depiction of Lear's madness, for he himself was gloomy of temperament, neurotic, and given to psychosomatic illnesses while composing. Might it not be more likely that he was troubled by Lear's feeling for Cordelia? The father–daughter relationship had a special meaning and emphasis for him, one which he was to explore most fully in *Rigoletto*, but which runs through his operas. Might not Lear have proved too overwhelming an exposition of it, or have led Verdi to too deep an exploration? If not, why did he not take advantage of the presence of both Lablache and Jenny Lind in London in 1847, and write for them the roles of Lear and Cordelia?

Whatever may have been his reason for deciding against *Lear*, after the première of *Macbeth* in Florence Verdi returned to the composition of *I masnadieri*. When he set out from Milan at the end of May, to travel to London via Paris, the opera was virtually finished except for the scoring. He took with him his young pupil Muzio. They travelled together from Milan to Paris by rail. coach and Rhine steamer, and Verdi stayed in Paris for a few days, sending Muzio ahead to London to find accommodation for them both. Verdi had heard a rumour that Jenny Lind did not want to sing in his opera, and he was determined not to put in an appearance in London until he was assured to the contrary. Muzio arrived on 3 June, and on the following day wrote to Barezzi in Busseto: 'What chaos London is! What confusion! Paris is nothing in comparison. People shouting, poor people weeping, steam engines flying along, men on horseback, in carriages, on foot, and all of them howling like the damned. My dear Signor Antonio, you can't imagine what it's like.'

By the time Verdi arrived, Muzio had found a suitable apartment. 'For three rooms I wanted to take, they asked £5 a week, and ten shillings for the maid. So I have taken only two rooms, and

I have had a bed put in the parlour for myself, which during the day turns into a most splendid divan.' A few days later, writing to Barezzi again, Muzio described Verdi's timetable in London: 'We get up at five in the morning, and we work until six in the evening, which is supper time. Then we go to the theatre for a while, and come back at eleven to go to bed, so as to be up early the next morning. The opera is progressing, two acts are already with the copyist, and the rest may be finished by next Monday.'

On 9 June Verdi wrote to Clarina Maffei in Milan:

I have been in London scarcely two days. I had a ghastly trip, but it amused me...In Paris I went to the Opéra. I have never heard more awful singers or a more mediocre chorus. The orchestra itself, if our lions will permit me to say so, was little better than mediocre. What I saw of Paris I quite liked, and above all I like the free life one can live in that country. I can say nothing about London because yesterday was Sunday and I haven't seen a soul. This smoke, however, and the smell of coal upset me. I feel as though I were on a steamboat all the time. In a few moments I'm going to the theatre to find out how my affairs are going. Emanuele, whom I sent ahead of me, has found me such a homœopathically minute suite of rooms that I can't move about in them. Nevertheless, it's quite clean, like all the houses in London.

I can't tell you how fanatical they are about Lind. They are already selling boxes and seats for tomorrow evening. I can't wait to hear her. My health is excellent. The journey didn't affect me very much because I took my time over it. It's true that I arrived late, so the impresario could complain, but if he says a single word to me that I don't care for, he'll get ten in reply and I shall leave immediately for Paris, regardless of the consequences.

As soon as it was known that he was in London, Verdi was invited everywhere. Lumley had placed a box at Her Majesty's Theatre at his disposal, and whenever he used it, as he did to hear Jenny Lind in Meyerbeer's *Robert le Diable*, he was the centre of attention. The ladies, a newspaper reported, 'devoured poor Verdi with their opera-glasses'.

54

But the single-minded composer refused most of the invitations he received, including one from Queen Victoria who had expressed a desire to meet him. He concentrated on finishing the scoring of the opera, plagued by the sore throat and stomach pains which he habitually suffered while composing. The weather, that summer, seems to have been unusually damp and misty, and this, according to Muzio, made Verdi even 'more eccentric and melancholy than usual'. But rehearsals with the singers began at the end of June, and proceeded fairly amicably. Verdi found himself liking Jenny Lind. 'She told me that she hates the theatre and the stage', wrote Muzio, 'and says she is unhappy and will not be content until she has no more to do with theatrical people and the theatre itself. In this regard, she is very much in accord with the Maestro's views. He, too, hates the theatre, and looks forward to retirement.'

On 17 July Verdi wrote to Clarina Maffei:

> You will be surprised to hear that I am still in London, and that the opera has not yet been staged. But the smoke and the fog are to blame, as well as this diabolical climate which robs me of all desire to work. But now, at last, everything is finished, or almost finished, and on Thursday 22nd the opera will definitely be staged. I have had two orchestral rehearsals, and if I were in Italy I would know by now whether the work was good or not, but here I understand nothing. Blame the climate... blame the climate!

On 22 July 1847 *I masnadieri* was given its first performance, by a cast which included Jenny Lind as Amalia, Italo Gardoni (Carlo), Filippo Coletti (Francesco) and Luigi Lablache (Count Moor). The occasion proved to be the highlight of the London season. At first reluctant to conduct the opera himself, Verdi agreed to do so on being petitioned by the Russian Ambassador and a deputation of English noblemen. The Queen and Prince Albert attended, as well as Prince Louis Bonaparte (soon to become Napoleon III), the

Left: Jenny Lind, the 'Swedish Nightingale'.

Filippo Coletti (baritone), who sang Francesco in the first production of I masnadieri.

Duke of Wellington and several other political and society figures. Muzio described the scene:

> The opera created a furore. From the Overture to the Finale there was nothing but applause, *evvivas*, recalls and encores. The Maestro himself conducted, sitting on a chair higher than the others, with baton in hand. As soon as he appeared in the orchestra pit, applause broke out, and continued for a quarter of an hour. Before it had finished, the Queen and Prince Albert her consort, the Queen Mother and the Duke of Cambridge, uncle of the Queen, the Prince of Wales, son of the Queen, and all the royal family and a countless number of lords and dukes had arrived. It suffices to say that the boxes were full of elegantly dressed ladies, and the pit so crowded that no one could remember having seen so many people there before. The doors had been opened at half past four, and the crowd had burst in with an enthusiasm never previously seen ... The Maestro was cheered, called on to the stage, both alone and with the singers, and pelted with flowers. All you could hear was 'Evviva Verdi! Bietifol [*sic*]'.

55

Verdi's account of the occasion was more laconic in tone ('Without having caused a furore, *I masnadieri* was well received'), and the press reviews were mixed, though generally favourable. *The Times* was less enthusiastic than the *Morning Post*, but the *Illustrated London News* thought the music was 'dramatic in the extreme and somewhat excels the masterpieces of Meyerbeer and other composers of the German romantic school'. But there were detractors. In the *Athenaeum*, Henry Chorley wrote: 'We take it to be the worst opera which has been given in our time at Her Majesty's Theatre!' Returning to the attack in a subsequent issue, he continued: 'Surely the question of our good (or bad) taste in rejecting Il Maestro as an authority is finally settled, and the field is left open for an Italian composer.'

The London correspondent of the Paris *Gazette Musicale*, already a confirmed anti-Verdian, published an unsympathetic report in the issue of 1 August:

> ... I will tell you frankly that I am of the opinion of the critics, who are far from regarding it as his *chef-d'œuvre*, and I have no need to tell you what I think in general of the *chefs-d'œuvre* of Verdi. Paris and London are unanimous in that respect: the *maestro* has succeeded no better in one city than in the other. It may be prejudice, bad taste, injustice, as certain people pretend; it may be so. I have no wish to contradict them. It is open to them to appeal to the future; I occupy myself only with the present time ... The musical system of Verdi is familiar to you; there does not exist an Italian composer more incapable of producing what is commonly called a melody.

After conducting the second performance of *I masnadieri*, Verdi handed the baton over to Balfe (composer of *The Bohemian Girl*) and then departed for Paris. It was from Paris that he wrote to friends in Milan of the delight he took in the city of London:

> No, it's not a city, it's a world. There's nowhere else to compare with it for size, richness, the beauty of the streets, the well-kept houses. You are struck dumb with astonishment and made to feel very humble when, in the midst of all these magnificent sights, you survey the Bank and the Docks. Who could resist such a nation? The surroundings and the country around London are wonderful. I'm not so keen on a number of the English customs: or, to be more exact, they don't suit us Italians. How ridiculous it is in Italy when some people imitate the English!

Lumley had asked Verdi to return to London as musical director of Her Majesty's Theatre, at a very large salary, and to compose for that theatre one opera per year for ten years. Insufficiently enthusiastic, Verdi proposed exorbitant terms ('ninety thousand francs for each season ... plus a house in the country and a carriage'), and nothing came of the offer. Whether he could have coped with the English temperament over a long period of time is doubtful. As Muzio wrote to Barezzi:

> Verdi aroused a decided furore in London, but the English are a formal and thoughtful people, and never give way to enthusiasm like the Italians, partly because they don't understand too well, and partly because they say educated people shouldn't make a row. The English go to the theatre to show off their riches and luxury; when an opera already printed is performed they have the score in hand and follow with their eyes what the singer does, and if, according to their ideas, the singer does well, they applaud and sometimes call for an encore; but they never insist, as our people do. I often went to hear the famous Rachel, the leading tragic actress. I saw some Englishmen with the printed tragedy in their hands, not looking at the actress, but watching to see if she said all the words.

The following year, 1848, *I masnadieri* was staged in Rome and Florence, and within the next five or six years it was seen in Barcelona, Madrid (newly orchestrated by one J. D. Skoczdopole), Rio de Janeiro, Havana, Malta, Lugano, Brussels, Venice, Smyrna, Budapest, Athens, Bucharest, Odessa, Buenos Aires, Milan and Vienna. The Budapest production in Italian was followed some months later by a production in Hungarian. So the opera can hardly be said to have failed. It was still being performed in Italy at the turn of the century, after which, like many another pre-*Rigoletto* Verdi opera, it languished until the Verdi revival in Austria and Germany, when it was heard for the first time in German at Bremen in 1928.

I masnadieri was the second of Verdi's four Schiller operas. *Giovanna d'Arco*, based loosely on *Die Jungfrau von Orleans*, had been staged in 1845, and *Luisa Miller* (1849) and *Don Carlos* (1867) were still to come. *Die Räuber*, Schiller's earliest play, is a long, sprawling piece written in an extraordinary prose that gathers up such diverse influences as Goethe, the Bible and demotic German speech into a new and heady style of its own. Schiller's brigands, or at any rate eight of them, are an interesting collection of villains, individually characterized. In Verdi's opera, they are reduced to the status of a chorus. Schiller's anti-hero, Karl von Moor, swearing vengeance on a society which he considers has wronged him, is really the victim of his own brother, and even more, of his own extravagant sensibility. A romantically restless youth, he progresses from the attitude of an adolescent disaffected with society to that of a conscienceless monster. From Jimmy Porter to Iago, one might say. At every stage in his career, he is given to moralizing about his condition. Similarly, his brother Franz, the villain, indulges in long philosophical justifications of his own misdeeds. Andrea Maffei's reduction of the play had to omit several scenes, most of the dialogue and the soliloquies, retaining only certain key sentences which, however, are meaningless torn from their original context. For instance, Maffei offers an Italian précis of Karl's opening lines about Plutarch ('Mir ekelt vor diesem tintenklecksenden Säkulum, wenn ich in meinem Plutarch lese von grossen Menschen'). In Schiller, the statement sparks off a long discussion with Spiegelberg, in which he tempts Karl towards the lawless life. Sung in recitative by Carlo, as the opening lines

of the opera ('Quando io leggo in Plutarco, ho noia, ho schifo di questa età d'imbelli'), the remark leads to nothing.

Something, but not much, of Schiller's manic-depressive Karl remains in Maffei's and Verdi's Carlo. In one of his finest long speeches in the play, Karl fulminates against Christian intolerance, covetousness and hypocrisy. It is an effective tirade whose opportunities the Verdi of *Don Carlos* or *La forza del destino* would have seized gratefully. The Verdi of *I masnadieri* was not ready for it. Another loss to the opera is Schiller's famous scene by the Danube at sunset, when, overcome by the glory of the setting sun, Karl bursts into an ecstasy of nostalgia for his childhood innocence, and longs to return to his mother's womb (though a little of this finds expression in Carlo's aria in the Bohemian forest scene of the opera). It is in this scene of the play that Karl expresses his gratitude to the entire gang of thieves for having saved him from capture. 'So wahr meine Seele lebt,' he swears, 'Ich will euch niemals verlassen' (As long as I live, I shall never forsake you). When urged not to swear so binding an oath, he repeats it vehemently. The strength of this scene makes somewhat more dramatically feasible the finale, in which Karl, unable to condemn Amalia to a life of shame, kills her. In the opera his action seems unclearly motivated and completely senseless.

Despite its admitted unevenness, and its disappointing libretto, *I masnadieri* is one of the most interesting, indeed one of the most inspired, of the works which emerged from those much maligned years in which Verdi obsessively chain-composed. He responded to Schiller's extremely Byronic hero even more strongly than to the authentic Byronic protagonist of his next opera, *Il corsaro*, and dressed Carlo and the other three principals in the most glorious melodies. The Prelude, an attractive, romantically melancholy *andante* for solo cello and orchestra, was written out of friendship for Alfredo Piatti, leader of the cello section in the orchestra at Her Majesty's, whom

Verdi had known during his student days in Milan. The arias for Jenny Lind were clearly tailored for her: some of the decoration looks and sounds as though Verdi added it to a vocal line initially conceived more plainly. But, if her arias somehow conjure up an earlier period, an earlier style of singing, the rest of *I masnadieri* does not. Structurally, Verdi may have been marking time, but what gives the opera its individuality and distinction is the tension between its darkly romantic arias and the jagged energy of its cabalettas. It succeeds by virtue of its combination of tunefulness and vigour. And like so much of early Verdi, it is an opera which, despite its faults, lodges itself securely in one's affections.

When Verdi left London for Paris after the second performance of *I masnadieri*, he was still seriously considering Lumley's offer of the musical directorship of Her Majesty's Theatre. But Francesco Lucca was now becoming more persistent, and it became clear to Verdi that the only immediate course open to him was to fulfil his contract with Lucca by composing the opera he had agreed to write. Sending Muzio on to Milan to make arrangements for the publication of *I masnadieri*, he remained in Paris for the remainder of the summer, and indeed was to make Paris his headquarters for the next two years.

Giuseppina Strepponi, the soprano who had helped to get Verdi's very first opera staged, and who had created the role of Abigaille in *Nabucco*, had retired from her operatic career in Italy and taken up residence in Paris to establish herself there as a teacher of singing. Verdi had probably called to see her on his way to London in June. He began to see her regularly on his return to Paris from London, and the beginning of their affair almost certainly dates from that summer of 1847. At first they lived apart, but in due course they began openly to live together. Approached by Paris for a new opera, Verdi agreed instead to

Giuseppina Strepponi in 1845.

revise *I Lombardi*, for which a new French text was prepared, in which the Lombard Crusaders became French Crusaders from Toulouse. The plot was altered somewhat, but as much as possible of its shape and emotional curve was retained, so that Verdi's musical revision consisted mainly of minor changes and rearrangement of the order of the numbers. He also composed some new pieces, including of course the obligatory ballet music. *Jérusalem*, as the opera was now called, was given a cool reception at the Opéra on 26 November 1847, but it was liked better when produced in the French provinces.

After *Jérusalem*, Verdi set to work on his opera for Lucca. The subject, Byron's poem *The Corsair*, had by now been agreed upon, and Piave had turned it into *Il corsaro*. By early February Verdi had finished work on the opera, and sent his score to Muzio in Milan, with instructions to deliver it to Lucca. Verdi appears, unusually for him, to have gone about the composition of the opera in a peculiarly cold-blooded manner, determined not to take too many pains over a work for 'that tiresome and ungrateful man'. What he eventually sent Lucca he would, in other circumstances, have considered merely a first draft to be revised. Normally, he would also have supervised rehearsals and conducted the first performances. In fact, he did not even attend the première in Trieste, in October. Instead he recommended Muzio to Lucca as producer and conductor, thus starting him on what was to prove a successful career as a conductor of opera. But the first performance of *Il corsaro* was only moderately successful, and at the end of the evening the only person to take a curtain-call was the scene designer. After productions in Milan (not at La Scala but at the Teatro Carcano), Venice and Malta, the opera disappeared for over a century, re-emerging on to the stage in Venice in 1963 and St Pancras, London, in 1966.

Piave's libretto for *Il corsaro* closely follows the events in Byron's poem, and on this occasion Verdi not only failed to hector his tame librettist, he even accepted without question what Piave provided. What he got was a surprisingly coherent libretto, whose verse may be undistinguished but whose structure is firm and compact. Byron's poem, written in heroic couplets and published in 1814, is one of his minor works, easy to read as Byron invariably is, but neither especially gripping as narrative nor particularly admirable as verse. The pirate chief Conrad (Corrado in the opera) is a typically Byronic creation. Both introvert and man of action, Corrado has opted out of society and taken to a life of adventure and excite-

Title-page of the vocal score of Gerusalemme, *the Italian translation of* Jérusalem.

ment, very like Carlo in *I masnadieri*. The last two lines of Byron's poem are known out of context—

> *He left a Corsair's name to other times,*
> *Link'd with one virtue, and a thousand crimes*

—but none of the music of Verdi's least-performed opera has been taken up by singers. This is a pity, for, though both musically and dramatically *Il corsaro* leaves much to be desired, much of its music is immensely enjoyable. If the opera as a whole mysteriously adds up to less than a sum of its parts, several of the parts themselves are well worth listening to. Medora's aria in the second scene of Act I has something of the

GERUSALEMME

OPERA IN QUATTRO ATTI

Musica del Maestro

GIUSEPPE VERDI

Prima Rappresentazione

DELLA NUOVISSIMA OPERA

IN TRE ATTI:

Il Corsaro

Parole di Fr. M. Piave. - Musica del Maestro G. Verdi

non mai esposta in altri Teatri.

PERSONAGGI

CORRADO, Capitano de' Corsari . . . . Fraschini Gaetano
GIOVANNI, Corsaro . . . . Volpini Giovanni
MEDORA, amante di Corrado . . . . Rapazzini Carolina
GULNARA, Schiava di Seid . . . . Barbieri-Nini Marianna
SEID, Pascià di Corone . . . . De Bassini Achille
SELIMO, Aga . . . . Petrovich Giovanni
EUNUCO, nero . . . . Cucchiari Francesco
Uno SCHIAVO . . . . Alberiazich Stefano

Cori e Comparse

Corsari - Guardie - Turchi - Schiavi - Odalische.

Lo Spettacolo incomincierà alle ore 7 1/2 precise.

NB. - I Signori Abbonati riceveranno i Libretti al Bigoncio.

al seno
Premer non cessa l'adorata Donna
Che a lui con mutue gemiti s'avvinghia

Playbill for the first production of Il corsaro *in Trieste, with an illustration from the opera.*

atmosphere of Leonora's first-act aria in *Il trovatore* five years later, and the orchestral introduction to the scene opens with an adumbration of the phrase which was to become the familiar 'Amami, Alfredo' in *La traviata*. The prison scene in Act III is expressive and delicately scored, and the trio with which the opera ends shows Verdi at his simplest and most effective. He was fond of ending with a trio (*I Lombardi, Ernani, I masnadieri*); his finest trio-finale of all, that for *La forza del destino*, was still several years away in the future.

It was in February 1848, the month in which Verdi completed *Il corsaro*, that revolution broke out in Paris, sparking off political uprising all over Europe. From Paris, Verdi wrote to Giuseppina Appiani in Milan:

You know all about what's going on in Paris. Since 24 February nothing has happened. The procession that accompanied the funeral of those killed to the memorial column of the Bastille was imposing, indeed magnificent, and although there were neither troops nor police

guards to maintain order, the whole thing passed without the slightest trouble. The big National Assembly to choose the government will meet on 20 April.... I can't conceal that I am enjoying myself very much, and that so far nothing has disturbed my dreams. I do nothing, go for walks, listen to meaningless gossip, buy nearly twenty newspapers a day (though, of course, I don't read them) to avoid being persecuted by the paper sellers, because when they see me coming with a bundle of newspapers in my arms, they don't offer me any. And I laugh and laugh and laugh.

Several months later, he wrote in more serious vein about the political situation to Clarina Maffei:

You want to know French public opinion about the events in Italy? Good Lord, what can I say to that? Those who are not against us are indifferent. I must say further that the idea of a united Italy frightens those little nobodies who are in power. It is certain that France will not intervene with arms unless some unforeseen event seems to force it in that direction. Anglo-French diplomatic intervention can be nothing but unfair, shameful for France and ruinous for us. Indeed, such intervention would tend to make Austria abandon Lombardy and content itself with Venetia. If Austria could be persuaded to give up Lombardy (at present this seems possible, though perhaps she would sack and burn everything before leaving), that would be a further dishonour for us, the devastation of Lombardy, and one more prince in Italy. No, no no: I have hopes neither of France nor of England. If I have hopes of anything, it is, can you imagine? of Austria: of confusion within Austria. Something serious must be emerging there, and if we know how to seize the moment and wage the war that should be waged, the war of insurrection, Italy could be free again. But God save us from having to rely on our kings or on foreign nations.

Between writing these two letters from Paris, one in March and the other in August, Verdi had made a quick visit to Milan. On 18 March news of a student uprising in Vienna had reached Milan. A crowd of Milanese congregated in front of the palace of the Austrian Governor, and the nervous guards fired on them. Thus began Milan's famous 'Cinque Giornate', 'Five Days' in which the citizens of Milan fought the Austrian soldiers. On the sixth day, the Austrians withdrew. Their general, Radetzky, had wanted to bombard the city but was restrained by the protests of the various foreign consuls in Milan. As soon as he heard of these events, Verdi hurried from Paris to Milan. The fighting was over by the time he arrived, but, stirred by the sight of the street barricades, he wrote to Piave in Venice: 'They can do what they like, they can intrigue as much as they like, those who seek to impose themselves by brute force, but they will not succeed in robbing the people of their rights. Yes, yes, only a few more years, perhaps only a few more months, before Italy is free, united and a republic.'

The fact that the Austrians, rather than destroy the entire city, had allowed themselves to be driven out of Milan did not mean the withdrawal of Austria from Northern Italy. The Milanese

appealed to Piedmont to come to their aid, and the Piedmontese reluctantly declared war on Austria. The Italian states, however, far from being united, began to quarrel among themselves about allegiances and pledges. When Carlo Alberto, King of Sardinia and Piedmont, drove the Austrians out of Venice, that city joyfully declared itself a republic. Nor had Milan any wish to annex itself to Piedmont. From the south of Italy a mood was afoot to unite all the Italian states, with the Pope as their temporal as well as spiritual head. Meanwhile the war between Austria and Northern Italy continued: there was to be no easy victory. Since Milan was no longer the centre of events, Verdi decided to return to Paris, to his unfinished business affairs and Giuseppina Strepponi—though not before purchasing a farm near Busseto, in the village of Sant' Agata. In due course, the Villa Sant' Agata, after several improvements had been made to it, was to become his and Giuseppina's home.

On his way back to Paris, in fact as he was crossing the Italian–Swiss border, Verdi wrote to Cammarano in Naples about an idea for an opera which had been suggested by Cammarano, an idea which linked up in his mind with a letter he had received the previous year from the poet Giuseppe Giusti urging him to place his music unequivocally at the service of the Republican cause. ('The kind of sorrow that now fills the minds of us Italians is the sorrow of a race that feels the need of a better destiny... Accompany, my Verdi, this high and solemn sorrow with your noble harmonies. Do what you can to nourish it, to strengthen it and direct it to its goal.')

Cammarano, more specifically and directly, had proposed the composition of a propaganda opera urging Italy to unite and expel the invader. His libretto took as its subject the defeat of Barbarossa, the German King and Holy Roman Emperor, in 1176 at the battle of Legnano, by the Italian cities which had combined to form the Lombard League. Cammarano knew that Italian audiences would understand *La battaglia di Leg-*

LA BATTAGLIA DI LEGNANO
MUSICA DI GIUSEPPE VERDI

The vocal score of La battaglia di Legnano.

nano to apply to the situation in 1848, although for censorship reasons he had to write about a war which had occurred seven centuries earlier. Verdi was enthusiastic about the project, and worked on the opera in Paris, where he and Giuseppina were now living together in a house they had rented in Passy. By the end of the year, Verdi had completed *La battaglia di Legnano*. His publisher Ricordi offered the opera to Rome, and it was, of course, accepted.

By the time Verdi arrived in Rome early in January 1849 to rehearse the opera, the city was in a state of political turmoil. Following the murder of his chief administrator by Republican extremists, the Pope had fled to Gaeta, a seaport town to the south of Rome, and outside the border

of the Papal State. In his absence the Republicans called a free election. The Pope, from his exile, made the mistake of condemning the election and forbidding Catholics to vote, and the result was therefore an overwhelming victory for the Republicans. The newly elected Assembly was to meet in February, and was expected to declare the Papal State a republic. On 27 January the Teatro Argentina was full to overflowing for the first performance of *La battaglia di Legnano*, and the atmosphere was charged with excitement. From its opening bars to its finale, Verdi's opera kept the entire audience in a state of hysterical enthusiasm. The Roman newspapers record that the first

words of the opening chorus, 'Viva Italia', were greeted with frenzied cries of 'Viva Verdi' and 'Viva Italia'. One newspaper reported that, when the hero of the opera leaped from a balcony in order to rejoin his regiment, a soldier in the fourth tier flung his overcoat and his epaulettes on to the stage, followed by all the chairs in his box, 'until the *carabinieri* came on the run and arrested him'. The entire last act, which is very short, was encored, not only on the first night but also at every subsequent performance of the season. After Rome, *La battaglia di Legnano* was performed in a few other Italian theatres, but with a libretto changed at the insistence of the censors. The Germans and Italians became Spaniards and Dutchmen, Barbarossa became the sixteenth-century Duke of Alba, and the new title was *L'assedio di Haarlem* (The Siege of Haarlem). But when it was revived in Parma in 1869, twenty years after its Roman première, the opera was topically subtitled *La disfatta degli Austriaci* (The Defeat of the Austrians). Italy had just won a decisive victory over Austria.

La battaglia di Legnano is not among those operas which in recent years have benefited by the revival of interest in early Verdi. Yet, both musically and dramatically, it is among the best of the composer's pre-*Rigoletto* works. Verdi and Cammarano may have intended to write a piece of pure and simple propaganda, but what they in fact produced turned out to be a valid work of art. The public story of the Lombard League's victory over Barbarossa and the private story of the Milanese warrior, his wife and his friend, are cleverly intertwined, and the score is full of music of stirring appeal. What is especially remarkable is the manner in which each succeeding scene is even more effective than the preceding one, generating an infectious and cumulative enthusiasm. This is an opera with an avowed purpose, to arouse the patriotic feelings of an oppressed people. The

Ronald Lewis (baritone) and Ronald Dowd (tenor) in the Welsh National Opera's modern-dress production of La battaglia di Legnano, *1960.*

historical situation which produced it, however, is irrelevant to a consideration of *La battaglia di Legnano* today. It fulfilled its propaganda purpose long ago, but it still has a valuable role to play as an enjoyable and effective piece of music-drama.

Though delighted with the success of his opera in Rome, Verdi did not personally enjoy being fêted as the composer of the Risorgimento, and left Rome to return to Paris and Giuseppina as soon as he decently could. The year 1849 was a disastrous one for the liberal cause in Italy: Austria won a victory over Piedmont in March, the Roman Republic collapsed in July, and Venice fell to the Austrians in August. 'Force still rules the world', Verdi wrote to a friend. 'And justice? What use is it against bayonets?' He and Giuseppina returned to Italy in August. Verdi had already agreed to compose another opera for Naples in collaboration with Cammarano, in order to help the librettist fulfil a commitment to the Teatro San Carlo. They had at first considered basing their opera on an historical novel by Francesco Guerrazzi, but, when this was rejected by the Neapolitan censors, Cammarano suggested that they should make use of Schiller's play, *Kabale und Liebe*, which Verdi had been considering earlier. Verdi quickly agreed, and Cammarano sent the first act of his libretto to the composer in Paris, who began to work on it immediately. The first two acts of the opera were written in Paris, and the final act was completed in Busseto, in a *palazzo* Verdi had rented while his property at nearby Sant' Agata was being improved. The citizens of Busseto were thrilled that their famous son should want to return to live amongst them, but they hardly knew how to react to the presence of a woman in his house. Giuseppina, intelligent, sensitive and kind-hearted, did her best not to exacerbate the situation, but Verdi, aloof and self-contained, tended to aggravate the locals by refusing to be sociable, which did not make Giuseppina's position any easier. By the time he left for Naples to rehearse *Luisa Miller*, accompanied by

his old friend Barezzi, some of the Bussetani were beginning to complain to one another about Verdi and his mistress from Paris.

Verdi had not accepted Cammarano's libretto for *Luisa Miller* without question or comment. As early as May, when he received a draft scenario, he had written:

> ... I confess to you I would have preferred two prima donnas, and I should also have preferred more emphasis on the prince's mistress, exactly as in Schiller. There would have been a contrast between her and Eloisa, and Rodolfo's love for Eloisa would have been more beautiful. I do realize, however, that I cannot always have what I want, and I am very pleased with it as it is. It seems to me, however, that all that devilish intrigue between Walter and Wurm, which dominates the whole of the play, doesn't here have the same colour and force that it has in Schiller. Perhaps in verse it will be different, but in any case let me know yourself whether you think I am right or not.

He continued with more general criticisms, and entreated Cammarano to develop further the duet in Act III for father and daughter: 'Make it a duet to bring tears to the eyes.' But Cammarano's final draft, reducing Schiller's five acts to three, does not appear to have incorporated all of Verdi's suggestions. Schiller had chosen the title of his play, *Kabale und Liebe* (Intrigue and Love), with care and deliberation. The play contrasts idealism and expediency, selfless romanticism and self-interested practicality, and the playwright's concern, beneath the trappings of romanticism, is in no sense romantic. His proposition is that love does not invariably triumph over all obstacles, and that the machinery of political intrigue can prove more than a match for the spirituality of romantic feeling. In reducing the play to a reasonable libretto length, Cammarano had naturally to make most of his excisions in the scenes of *Kabale* rather than in those of *Liebe*, love being simple while intrigue is complex.

Verdi and Antonio Barezzi arrived in Naples

Cover of the vocal score of Luisa Miller.

G. VERDI.

LUISA MILLER

Opera completa
per
Canto
e
Pianoforte

Edizioni Ricordi

after having been delayed for two weeks in Rome by quarantine regulations due to an outbreak of cholera. Rome was under French occupation, and Verdi wrote to his French agent, Léon Escudier:

> The affairs of our country are desolating. Italy is now no more than a vast and beautiful prison! If only you could see this pure sky, this mild climate, this sea, these mountains, this beautiful city!! To the eyes, a paradise, but to the heart an inferno!! The rule of your fellow countrymen in Rome is no better than that of the rest of Italy. The French try to win the favour of the Romans, who have so far remained very dignified and firm.

While they were in Naples, Verdi took his ex-father-in-law to see Herculaneum, Pompeii, the island of Ischia and several other places of interest. The première of *Luisa Miller* had been postponed to 8 December, because of Verdi's late arrival; Barezzi, who had to return to Busseto before that date, nevertheless had a chance to attend rehearsals.

At the beginning of the rehearsal period, Verdi had an absurd quarrel with the management of the Teatro San Carlo. Cammarano had warned him that the theatre's financial situation was unsound, and advised him to demand his fee before parting with the score of *Luisa Miller*. The directors of the theatre demanded that he hand over the score, but made no offer to pay for it and threatened to have the composer arrested if he attempted to leave Naples without official permission. Verdi refused to be intimidated, and announced that he would take himself and his score on board one of the French warships in the Bay of Naples and demand protection. The authorities backed down, but Verdi was left with a sense of grievance. A week after the first performance of *Luisa Miller* he left Naples, vowing that he would never produce another opera in that city. As it happened, he never did, although he was to enter into negotiations with the San Carlo more than once.

The première of *Luisa Miller* was successful, and so was the Rome production some months later. The opera is still quite frequently performed, though it has never become a general favourite. It is an important transitional work, marking both the end of Verdi's first period and the beginning of his second. (This second period might be considered to reach as far as *Aida*, with the Requiem and the last two Shakespeare operas constituting the composer's third creative period.) The change can almost be pin-pointed as occurring between Acts II and III of *Luisa Miller*, whose first two acts belong to the world of Bellini and Donizetti, a world which Verdi leaves with the tender regret of the tenor aria in Act II, 'Quando le sere al placido', while Act III is both a real anticipation of the musical style and dramatic atmosphere of *La traviata* and a confident assertion of Verdi's by now complete independence from the past. It is interesting and touching to note that, many years later, Arrigo Boito, who was to collaborate with the elderly Verdi, wrote of the aria 'Quando le sere al placido': 'Ah, if you knew the kind of echo and ecstasy that this divine cantilena awakens in the soul of an Italian, especially in the soul of one who has sung it from his earliest youth!'

After the first three performances of *Luisa Miller*, Verdi made his way back to Busseto, travelling from Naples to Genoa by boat and on by coach to Busseto where Giuseppina Strepponi was awaiting him. He was back in time for Christmas: by the beginning of the new year, 1850, he was already suggesting to Cammarano new ideas for operas. While in Naples he had asked that Victor Hugo's play *Le Roi s'amuse* should be brought to the librettist's attention. Now he wrote to suggest *El Trovador*, by the Spanish playwright Garcia Gutiérrez. 'It seems to me very fine, rich in ideas and strong situations.' These two plays were in due course to become *Rigoletto* and *Il trovatore*, though Cammarano was to be involved only with the latter one. Meanwhile, Verdi had signed a contract with his publisher Ricordi by which he agreed to compose a new opera in November in any one of the leading Italian theatres 'except La Scala, Milan'. Leaving Cammarano to consider future projects he turned to Piave for a libretto, while Ricordi began negotiations to have the opera produced in Trieste.

Piave recommended a French play, *Le Pasteur*, by Emile Souvestre and Eugène Bourgeois, which he had seen staged in Italian as *Stiffelius*. The play, first produced in Paris two years earlier, dealt with the floundering marriage of a contemporary German Protestant clergyman whose wife had committed adultery. This was not an easy subject for Italian audiences to understand: a priest with a wife, a husband who considers it Christian to forgive marital infidelity, these were stumbling-blocks to their enjoyment of Verdi's score. There were also the usual censorship difficulties. A scene in church, in which the clergyman quotes the New Testament, was considered to be blasphemous and was severely mutilated, and in the penultimate scene the wife was not allowed to address her husband as 'ministro' or confess to him as a priest of the Church.

Although some (but not all) of the first perform-ances in Trieste omitted the offending third act, *Stiffelio* was well received. However, for its production some months later in Rome and Florence, and for subsequent productions in Catania, Palermo and Naples, the censorship authorities insisted on several changes. The clergyman became prime minister of a German principality, the action was moved back in time to the beginning of the fifteenth century, and the opera was renamed *Guglielmo Wellingrode*. After the first performance of *Stiffelio* in Trieste, a critic had written: 'This is a work at once religious and philosophical, in which sweet and tender melodies follow one another in the most attractive manner, and which achieves... the most moving dramatic effects without having recourse to bands on the stage, choruses, or superhuman demands on vocal cords or lungs.' In other words, *Stiffelio* was an extension of Verdi's new *Luisa Miller* manner. But it did not survive, and six years later he revised it, fitting much of the music to a new libretto.

Illustration from the cover of the original vocal score of Stiffelio.

4 Opera as Drama:
Rigoletto, Il Trovatore, La Traviata

As soon as *Stiffelio* had been staged, Verdi began to discuss his next opera with Piave. He had been asked by the Teatro la Fenice to provide a new work to be staged in February 1851. This was now only two or three months away. He had drawn Piave's attention to *Kean* by the elder Dumas, a play about the great English actor Edmund Kean. This would surely have made a fascinating Verdi opera, but the play finally decided upon was Victor Hugo's *Le Roi s'amuse* which Verdi had some time earlier mentioned to Cammarano. Piave had assured Verdi that the censorship authority would raise no objection to this as a subject, and he began to work on the libretto. Set in the court of the libertine François I of France, the play tells of the King's abduction of the daughter of his hunchback jester, and of the jester's revenge. In Verdi's opinion the play was 'perhaps the greatest drama of modern times', and Tribolet, the jester, 'a creation worthy of Shakespeare'. But the play had caused a scandal at its première in Paris in 1832, and had forthwith been banned. It can hardly have surprised Verdi when the censor's office objected to its use as an operatic subject for Venice, condemning the play as immoral and obscene. The censor's real though unstated objection was to a reigning monarch being shown as debauched and, even worse, being assassinated.

Piave was willing to recast his libretto along lines suggested by the censors, but Verdi rejected his librettist's revisions, and stated his attitude in a letter to C. D. Marzari, President of the Fenice's board of management:

> In order to reply immediately to yours of the 11th, let me say I have had very little time to examine the new libretto. I have seen enough, however, to know that in its present form it lacks character, significance, and, in short, the

dramatic moments leave one completely cold. If it was necessary to change the characters' names, then the locality should have been changed as well. You could have a Duke or Prince of some other place, for example a Pier Luigi Farnese, or put the action back to a time before Louis XI when France was not a united kingdom, and have a Duke of Burgundy or Normandy etc. etc., but in any case an absolute ruler. In the fifth scene of Act I, all that anger of the courtiers against Triboletto doesn't make sense. The old man's curse, so terrifying and sublime in the original, here becomes ridiculous because his motive for uttering the curse doesn't have the same significance, and because it is no longer a subject who speaks in so forthright a manner to his King. Without this curse, what scope or significance does the drama have? The Duke has no character. The Duke must definitely be a libertine: without this there is no justification for Triboletto's fear that his daughter might leave her hiding-place, and the drama is made impossible. What would the Duke be doing in the last act, alone in a remote inn, without an invitation, without a rendezvous? I don't understand why the sack has gone. Why should a sack matter to the police? Are they worried about the effect? But let me say this: why do they think they know better than I do about this? Who is playing the Maestro? Who can say this will make an effect and that won't? We had this kind of difficulty with the horn in *Ernani*. Well, did anyone laugh at the sound of that horn? With that sack removed, it is improbable that Triboletto would talk for half an hour to a corpse, before a flash of lightning reveals it to be his daughter. Finally, I see that they have avoided making Triboletto an ugly hunchback!! A hunchback who sings? Why not?... Will it be effective? I don't know. But, I repeat, if I don't know then they who propose this change don't know either. I thought it would be beautiful to portray this extremely deformed and ridiculous character who is inwardly passionate and full of love. I chose the subject precisely because of these qualities and these original traits, and if they are cut I shall no longer be able to set it to music. If anyone says to me I can leave my notes as they are for this new plot, I reply that I don't understand this kind of thinking, and I say frankly that my music, whether beautiful or ugly, is never written in a vacuum, and that I always try to give it character.

To sum up, an original, powerful drama has been turned into something ordinary and cold. I am extremely sorry that the Management did not reply to my last letter. I can only repeat and beg them to do what I asked then, because my artist's conscience will not allow me to set this libretto to music.

Eventually, on 25 January, a mere four weeks before the opera was due to be performed, a compromise solution was reached. The situations in Victor Hugo's play were retained, but the scene was changed from the French court of François I to that of the Duke of Mantua. A document drawn up at Verdi's house in Busseto, and signed by him, by Piave and by the Fenice's secretary, lists the points agreed, among them that 'in the scene in which the sack containing the corpse of Triboletto's daughter appears, Maestro Verdi reserves to himself the right to make such changes as he considers necessary'. The hunchback remained a hunchback but, having already had his name italianized from Tribolet to Triboletto, he finally became Rigoletto (presumably from the French 'rigoler', meaning 'to guffaw').

Because of the delay caused by the fight with the censors, the first night was postponed for some weeks, and *Rigoletto* finally reached the stage on 11 March 1851. One often reads that Verdi must therefore have composed the opera in forty days, but in fact much of the music had been in his head for several months of 1850, and parts of it had already been written down. Much of the opera was composed at the Palazzo Orlandi in Busseto, where Verdi and Giuseppina Strepponi were still living. Verdi's parents had stayed with them over Christmas, but they were unable to accept his illicit relationship with Giuseppina, and this led

PUBLIÉ PAR EUGÈNE RENDUEL.

M DCCC XXXII.

Cover of the first edition of Victor Hugo's play Le Roi s'amuse, *on which* Rigoletto *is based.*

to friction between parents and son. In addition, Verdi was annoyed with his father, who he thought was meddling in the management of his farming properties. In February, therefore, he purchased for his parents a farm at Vidalenzo, not far from Sant' Agata, and had a legal document drawn up setting out the terms on which he was willing to support his mother and father. They were to receive the farm and an annual income, but Verdi made it clear that he wanted no interference from them, either in his personal life or in his business affairs.

In February Verdi went to Venice to begin rehearsing *Rigoletto*. There was a difficulty over the casting of the contralto role of Maddalena, for the Fenice's contraltos were unwilling to undertake

Rigoletto: *scene from a production in Brno, with* (left) *part of Verdi's first draft of the opening scene and* (right) *costume designs for an early production at La Scala.*

so small a part with no solo aria. But a Maddalena was, in due course, found, and rehearsals proceeded. Fearing that one of the Duke of Mantua's arias was so catchy a tune that it could too easily become known and sung all over Venice before the première, and thus fail to make its dramatic effect in the opera, Verdi withheld 'La donna è mobile' from the tenor until the day before the dress rehearsal. He was surely right to exercise such caution, for the whole of Venice was singing the tune immediately after the première.

Rigoletto was acclaimed as a masterpiece by audiences from the very beginning, although it confused a number of professional critics by not being formally what they considered a serious opera should be. Soon after its Venice première, it was being staged all over Italy, although in order to circumvent various local religious or political censors it had to be presented in a number of different guises. In Rome it was *Viscardello*, in Naples *Clara di Perth* at its first production, and *Lionello* five years later. As *Rigoletto*, the opera's fame spread rapidly, and it was soon produced wherever there were opera houses, sometimes in Italian but also in German, French, English, Hungarian, Polish, Spanish, Russian, Croatian, Swedish, Norwegian and Danish. Eventually it was translated also into Slovenian, Finnish, Bulgarian, Serbian, Estonian, Lettish, Lithuanian and Hebrew. Victor Hugo, disconcerted by the success of Verdi's opera compared with that of his own play, greatly resented its popularity, and for six years managed to prevent its production in Paris. When he eventually heard *Rigoletto*, he was forced to admit its greatness, though his comment on the celebrated quartet in Act IV reads ambiguously: 'If only I could make four characters in my play speak simultaneously, and have the audience grasp the words and sentiments, I would obtain the very same effect.'

No one doubts today either that *Rigoletto* is one of the great masterpieces of opera or that, formally, it marks another huge step forward for Verdi. But at the time of the first performances,

although audiences responded enthusiastically, the more traditionally minded among the music critics voiced their fear that Verdi's wonderful melodic gift, with which they had formerly been slow to credit him, was now beginning to fail. The scene in which Rigoletto is first accosted by the assassin Sparafucile was cited as an example— that scene with its extraordinary melody in the orchestra, above which the dialogue of the two voices, baritone and bass, moves with such freedom and dramatic realism. *Rigoletto* is virtually a treasure-house of melody, though there are fewer arias than in any of Verdi's earlier operas, for he conceived the work as a series of duets. To emphasize the formal innovations in *Rigoletto*, however, is to do the opera an injustice, for what is most remarkable about it is its sustained level of inspiration. Never quick to bow to the demands of his singers, Verdi now possessed the confidence to go his own way completely. When the soprano who was to sing Gilda in the first Rome production of *Rigoletto* requested him to insert a new aria for her, he made it clear that he was not willing to tamper with his score in any way. Any new number, he pointed out, would be superfluous. 'And where would it be put? Words and music can be written, but would make no effect if not in the right time and place.' He had composed *Rigoletto* as one long series of duets because that was how he wanted to do it. 'If anyone comments "But you could have done this or that or the other", I can only say "That may be, but I did not know how to do it any better".'

It is Verdi's skilful use of his orchestra, his brilliant delineation of the characters, including the minor ones, as well as his prodigality of melodic invention and the advance he makes towards integral structure, which result in *Rigoletto* being one of the most popular operas as well as one of the finest. It is positively Mozartian in its humanity, and there can be no higher praise than that.

As usual, Verdi returned home to Busseto as soon as possible after the first performances of his

Above: Verdi's villa at Sant'Agata.
Left: Part of the grounds of the villa.

opera. *Rigoletto* was safely launched, but he had both personal and professional problems to face. The conventionally minded, in Busseto and beyond it, were distressed that the leading composer of the day should choose such *louche* subjects for his operas, and those who knew of his relationship with Giuseppina Strepponi disapproved of that too. Life for Giuseppina in Busseto, especially when Verdi was away rehearsing a new opera, cannot have been easy, for most of the townsfolk refused to have anything to do with her, and she did not get on at all with Verdi's parents. In June 1851, Verdi's mother died, which distressed him greatly. Later in the year Verdi and Giuseppina went to Paris; while they were there, the composer received a letter from his old benefactor and ex-father-in-law, putting to him, among other things, the question which the whole of Busseto would love to have asked. Why did Verdi not legalize his union with the woman he was keeping? Barezzi's letter is lost, but Verdi's reply, written from Paris in January 1852, is a fascinating document:

Dearest Father-in-law,

After all these years, I never expected to receive so cold a letter from you, and one with, unless I am mistaken, some very harsh words. If this letter had not been signed 'Antonio Barezzi', that is, my benefactor, I should have replied abruptly or not at all. But since it bears a name which I shall always respect, I shall do my best to attempt to convince you that I have not merited your reproach. To do this I must go back to the past, speak of others, of our home town, so my letter will be somewhat long and boring, though I shall try to be as brief as possible.

I do not believe that you would have written to me of your own accord, a letter which you knew could only distress me. But you live in a town whose inhabitants unfortunately enjoy meddling in the affairs of others and disapproving of everything that does not conform to their ideas. I make a point of not interfering, un-invited, in the affairs of others, and I demand in return that no one interfere in mine. This is what has caused the gossip, the whisperings and disapproval. I have the right to expect in my own country the same freedom of action that is allowed in less civilized places. Judge for yourself, severely, yet coldly and dispassionately. What harm is there in my living in isolation, in my preferring not to pay calls on titled people, or refraining from partaking in the festivities and joys of others? Or if I manage my own properties because it pleases me to do so? I repeat, what harm is there in that? In any case, no one else is any the worse for it.

Having said this, I come now to the sentence in your letter: 'I realize that the time has passed when I could be entrusted to handle your business, but I am still able to be useful in smaller matters...' If by that you mean that I used to turn to you with serious problems, but now ask your help only with trifling matters, such as the letter enclosed with yours, I can find no justification for that criticism. Though, if the situation were reversed, I would do whatever you wanted, I can only say that this will be a lesson to me

for the future. If your sentence is a reproach to me for not putting my affairs in your hands while I am away, allow me to ask you: how could I be so indiscreet as to place so heavy a burden on you, when you yourself never ever set foot in your own fields, but leave everything to your capable staff? Should I have bothered Giovannino? But is it not true that, last year, when I was in Venice, I gave him full power of attorney and he never once went to Sant' Agata? I do not say this as a reproach to him. He was perfectly correct. He had important enough business of his own to attend to, and therefore no time to spare for mine.

So much for my opinions, actions and for my life—I was about to say my public life. And while we are making revelations, I have no objection to raising the curtain which veils the mysteries enclosed within four walls, and tell you about my home life. I have nothing to hide. There lives in my house a lady, free and independent, who, like myself, prefers a solitary life, and in possession of a fortune that caters for all her needs. Neither I nor she is obliged to account to anyone for our actions. But who knows what our relations are? What affairs? What ties? What rights I have over her or she over me? Who knows whether she is my wife or not? And if she is, who knows what the reasons may be for not publicly announcing the fact? Who knows whether that is a good or a bad thing? Might it not be a good thing? And even if it is a bad thing, who has the right to ostracize us? I will say this, however: in my house she is entitled to as much respect as myself, more even. And no one is allowed to forget that for any reason. And finally, she has every right, both because of her conduct and her character, to that consideration she habitually shows to others.

This long and rambling letter is meant only to say that I claim that freedom of action to which everyone is entitled. My nature rebels against conforming to the prejudices of others; and you, who are so good, so just, and with so great a heart, must not let yourself be influenced by the gossip of a town which, in my opinion— I must say this—some time ago would not deign to appoint me as its organist, and now whispers calumnies against me. This cannot go on, but if it does I shall know how to defend myself. The world is very big, and the loss of twenty or thirty thousand francs will not stop me from choosing

some other part of it to live in. There should
be nothing in this letter to give offence to you,
but if anything should, then please consider it
not written, for I swear on my honour it is not
my intention to offend you. I have always
thought of you as my benefactor, and I continue, with pride, to do so. Farewell, farewell.
With friendship as ever.

Verdi's letter is not without its disingenuous
aspects. He was not married to Giuseppina, and
they were not to marry until 1859, seven years
later. Yet the life they lived together was that of
a respectable married couple. It is possible that
Verdi found the religious ceremony distasteful, for
he was an agnostic in religious matters, and no
friend of the clergy, though he had married his first
wife in a church. The story that he had promised

Left above: Costume design by Filippo Sanjust for Azu-cena in the Visconti production of Il trovatore *at Covent Garden.*
Left below: Finale of Act II of the English National Opera production of Il trovatore.
Above: Verdi's study at Sant'Agata.

his dying wife he would never marry again, and that Strepponi admitted this to a friend, can neither be proved nor disproved.

By the time Verdi and Strepponi went to Paris for the winter of 1851–2, Verdi's next opera was under way. He and Cammarano chose the Spanish play by Gutiérrez which became *Il trovatore*. The opera had not been commissioned: Verdi had suggested it to Cammarano because he was impressed by the play, and when the librettist died in Naples in July 1852, leaving about one-third of the libretto still to be written, Verdi engaged Leone Emanuele Bardare, a young Neapolitan poet, to complete it. He had intended to offer the opera to Naples because of Cammarano's connection with the Teatro San Carlo, but his main concern was to have it produced by whichever

theatre had the most suitable singers, and he finally agreed to allow *Il trovatore* to be staged at the Apollo Theatre, Rome, in January 1853.

While he had been in Paris he had signed a contract to write a new work for production at the Opéra, and when he arrived back in Busseto he began to correspond with Piave concerning another opera for Venice. By the time he came to produce *Il trovatore* in Rome he was also composing the Venice opera, *La traviata*, which was given its première a mere six weeks after *Il trovatore*.

Audiences in Rome immediately recognized *Il trovatore* as the masterpiece it is, though some of the critics thought that Verdi was killing the art of *bel canto* by the impossible demands he made on his singers. Despite the melodramatic improbabilities of its plot *Il trovatore* soon became, and has remained ever since, one of the most popular of all operas. Its effects are broad and immediate, and to us nowadays it seems the veritable apotheosis of the *bel canto* opera with its wealth of melody and its demands for vocal beauty, agility and range. The muscular energy, the almost brutal

vigour and speed of the opera are remarkable, and its covert temperamental references to the turmoil of the composer's own life at the time of its composition are unmistakable. Verdi's grief at the death of his mother found its way into the portrayal of the gypsy Azucena. 'People say the opera is too sad, and that there are too many deaths in it,' Verdi wrote to Clarina Maffei, 'but, after all, death is all there is in life. What else is there?'

Verdi returned by sea via Genoa to Busseto, to find his villa at Sant' Agata ready for occupation. He and Giuseppina moved in: it was to be their home for the rest of their lives. There were still several additions and alterations to be made to it, which proceeded slowly over the years, and Giuseppina complained to Clarina Maffei: 'I can-

La traviata: *Josephine Barstow as Violetta, and (inset) a design from the first edition.*

LA TRAVIATA
Libretto di Francesco Maria Piave
MUSICA DI
GIUSEPPE VERDI
CAVALIERE DELLA LEGION D'ONORE
dall' Editore TITO DI GIO. RICORDI dedicata
in segno di stima ed amicizia all' egregio signor Dottore
CESARE VIGNA

Cover of the vocal score of La traviata.

not tell you how frequently, during the building operations, the beds, wardrobes and furniture danced from room to room. It is sufficient to say that, apart from the kitchen, cellar and stables, we have slept and eaten in every corner of the house.'

With only weeks before the première of *La traviata* in Venice, Verdi devoted himself wholeheartedly to its completion. He and Giuseppina were both unwell, and the last act with the dying Violetta was written in an atmosphere of gloom which was highly suitable to its content. Verdi was nervous about the singers engaged, especially the soprano, Fanny Salvini-Donatelli, of whom he had heard discouraging reports. Piave, who was staying at Sant' Agata, was instructed to convey to the Teatro la Fenice Verdi's conviction that unless a new cast was found the opera would fail. The weather at Sant' Agata played its part in adding to the general air of pessimism. 'When it

rains', wrote Piave to the Fenice's Secretary, 'I assure you it's a case of looking at oneself in the mirror to see if one is still in human form, or whether one hasn't been turned into a toad or a frog.'

Verdi wanted the management of the Fenice to replace Salvini-Donatelli with Rosina Penco, his *Trovatore* Leonora from Rome, but she was not available and the date by which Verdi was entitled to demand a change of soprano had already passed. He was stuck with Salvini-Donatelli. When he received an anonymous letter from Venice, warning him that unless at least two of the three principals were replaced the performance would be a disaster, Verdi gloomily passed it on to Piave, adding: 'I know, I know.' He arrived in Venice on 21 February to orchestrate the opera and to rehearse it, and a mere thirteen days later, on 6 March 1853, *La traviata* was given its first performance. The audience laughed throughout the last act, as the extremely stout and healthy-looking soprano fought to convince them she was dying of consumption. The tenor was in poor voice, and the baritone, Felice Varesi, who, as Verdi's first Macbeth and Rigoletto, ought by this time to have trusted the composer, thought his role was unworthy of him and merely 'walked through' it.

The morning after the first performance, Verdi wrote a laconic note to Muzio: 'Dear Emanuele, *La traviata* last night—fiasco. Was the fault mine or that of the singers? Time will be the judge.' To Angelo Mariani, who was to conduct Verdi's *Aroldo* four years later, he asserted that he was not upset by the verdict of the audience, and added: 'I myself believe that the last word on *La traviata* was not heard last night. They will hear it again—and we shall see! Meanwhile, dear Mariani, note the fiasco.'

One of the reasons Verdi had been drawn to *La Dame aux Camélias*, which he had seen in Paris the previous year when it was first produced, was that it dealt with a contemporary subject, for Marie Duplessis, the original of Dumas' Marguerite

Giuseppe Verdi. A portrait by an unknown artist.

*A portrait by an unknown artist of Giuseppina Strepponi
holding the score of* Nabucco.

A scene from the Budapest production of I Lombardi
which was seen at Covent Garden in 1976.

Above: Cornell MacNeill (baritone) as Rigoletto in the 1966 Royal Opera House production.   *Below: Tito Gobbi (baritone) in the title-role of* Falstaff *at the Royal Opera House, Covent Garden.*

Above: Costume designs by David Walker for the English National Opera's La traviata.

Below: Joan Sutherland as Violetta in La traviata, *Royal Opera House, Covent Garden.*

A scene from the Visconti production of Don Carlos *at the Royal Opera House, Covent Garden.*

Above: A scene from the first French-language production of Aida *in Paris, 1880.*

Below: The triumphal scene from Aida *in the Covent Garden production of 1968.*

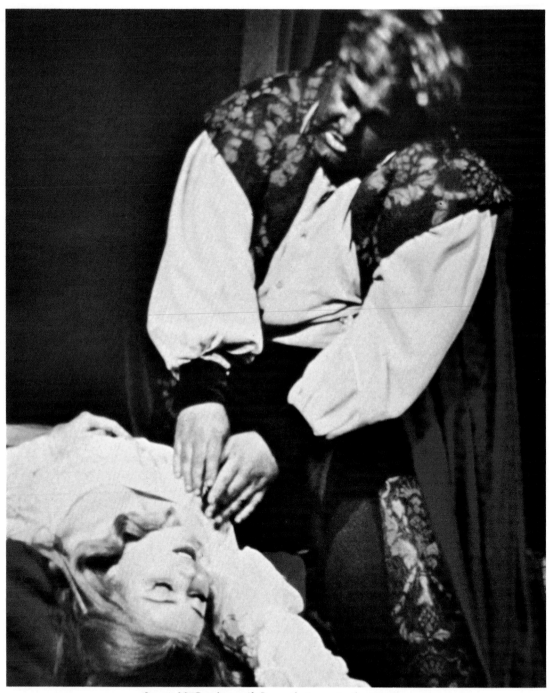

*James McCracken and Gwyneth Jones in the Covent
Garden production of* Otello.

A caricature showing La traviata *being rejected by a French critic.*

Gautier, had died only four years earlier. But when Verdi's operatic version reached the stage the action had been moved back to the early eighteenth century, and the *décor* and costumes were those of Louis XIV. It is curious that Verdi should have agreed to this, for while he was composing the opera he had written to a friend: 'A subject from our own time. Another person would not perhaps have composed it because of the costumes, because of the period, because of a thousand other foolish objections, but I am delighted with the idea.' He must have been overruled by the Fenice management with its strange ideas of propriety and the dignity of its theatre.

Verdi's letters about the fiasco were written before any of the newspaper reviews had appeared. The reviews, though mixed, were by no means entirely unfavourable. The critic of the *Gazzetta di Venezia*, after praising the orchestral performance and several numbers in the opera whose first act he found 'full of beauties worthy of the palmy days of Rossini', refused to judge the opera as a whole until he had heard a better performance. The Venice correspondent of the Milan *Gazzetta Musicale* called it 'a worthy product of that inexhaustible genius which has given to Europe *Nabucco, Ernani, Rigoletto*', and the last act 'a perfect jewel from the very beginning of that tender prelude on the violins which so piteously prepares us for the tragic catastrophe'.

Ten performances of *La traviata* were given, but for more than a year the opera was not staged anywhere else, for Verdi was unwilling to allow another production unless he could personally supervise it. He toyed with the idea of producing it in Rome, but was forestalled by a request from Venice to allow the opera to be staged again there. The request came, not from the Fenice but from the Teatro San Benedetto, a theatre smaller than the Fenice but almost equally distinguished. The impresario offered to engage the finest singers available, with Piave to direct the production, and to allow unlimited rehearsal time. The Louis XIV period, however, was to be adhered to, for apparently it would have been tempting providence to show contemporary life on the operatic stage; it was to be many years before the opera was produced in mid-nineteenth-century costume. After an initial hesitation, Verdi gave his consent to this second Venice production, and the Venetians heard *La traviata* again on 6 May 1854. This time the opera was an overwhelming success, a success which immediately spread. *La traviata* was produced in many other Italian towns and in several other countries, and was soon the most talked-about opera of its day. Verdi was pleased with its reception at the Teatro San Benedetto, but could not help remarking that it was the same audience listening to the same opera.

There are curious parallels between *La traviata* and Verdi's own domestic situation, as there were also between the personal life of Alexandre Dumas the Younger and his *Dame aux Camélias*. Not so curious perhaps in the case of Dumas, for it was because he had been a lover of Marie Duplessis, the famous Parisian courtesan who died of consumption at the age of twenty-three, that he wrote his novel and later adapted it for the stage. Armand Duval, who shares his creator's initials, was clearly intended as a self-portrait, for Dumas' first meeting with Marie Duplessis had taken place in conditions similar to those in which Marguerite and Armand meet in novel and play,

and Dumas had lived with Marie in the country outside Paris during the summer of 1845. Perhaps one of the reasons Verdi was drawn to *La Dame aux Camélias* was that he saw in it something of the emotional truth of his own situation. Giuseppina was no courtesan, but she was the mother of two illegitimate children from an earlier relationship. (One, a boy, is known to have been alive in 1849, aged eight. The other may have died in infancy.) And Verdi may have considered Barezzi an equivalent of the elder Germont. It is certainly true that *La traviata* occupied a special place in Verdi's affections, and that it is a much more intimate and personal work than anything else he had written. Asked at this time which of his operas he liked best, Verdi replied that as a professional he preferred *Rigoletto*, but as an amateur *La traviata*.

What is especially remarkable about *La traviata* is the way in which its separate musical numbers arise from and merge into the general melodic background. Each of its four acts has a structural unity which is so apparent in performance that the opera could almost be described as a four-movement symphony for voices and orchestra. Not only is it one of Verdi's finest and best-loved operas, it is also one of the world's great music dramas. That it was not immediately given credit for its musico-dramatic qualities can only have been because of its immense wealth of melody. Much of its atmosphere of pathos derives from Verdi's extraordinarily expressive writing for the string section of the orchestra. Each of the great operas of his maturity has its own distinctive sound, and in *La traviata* the dark, melancholy hues of *Il trovatore* have given way to a warmer string sound, vibrant with pathos. The opera is so familiar to audiences today, its melodies so much a part of every opera-goer's experience, that it is not easy to stand back sufficiently from the work to appraise it freshly. It is an opera in which all of Verdi's greatest gifts are deployed: his technical mastery, his clarity, his humanity, his psychological penetration, his sense of theatre and his unerring taste.

5 Patriot and Politician: Les Vêpres Siciliennes to La Forza del Destino

After the initial *Traviata* 'fiasco', Verdi had returned to Sant' Agata and begun searching for possible subjects for the Paris opera he had agreed to compose. *Faust* was suggested to him, but was rejected ('I adore *Faust*, but I don't wish to set it to music. I have studied it a thousand times, but I don't find the character of Faust musical'). A Venetian lawyer and playwright, Antonio Somma, suggested a number of subjects. These too were rejected, but Verdi in his turn suggested to Somma that they might collaborate on *King Lear*, informing him that he preferred Shakespeare to all other playwrights. Verdi had already made his own detailed synopsis of the play, and now Somma began to write a complete libretto, in close consultation with Verdi, who advised him every step of the way. For the next two years the two men continued to correspond, with Verdi making detailed criticisms, scene by scene, and continually checking Somma's tendency to expand. 'In the theatre', he told Somma, '"long" is synonymous with "boring", and the boring is the worst of all styles.' Eventually Somma finished his libretto, and Verdi paid him for it, but by this time Verdi had decided on a different opera for Paris, so *King Lear* was once again put aside. 'Perhaps it's just as well, for I shall be able to devote myself to it later with all the necessary leisure, and I shall make, I don't say something new, but something a little different from the others.'

The summer of 1853 was passed pleasantly at Sant' Agata. In addition to his correspondence with Antonio Somma and others, Verdi had plenty of work to do on his farm which he operated at a profit, largely from the sale of cattle. But he liked to get away from Sant' Agata for the winter, and in October, shortly after his fortieth birthday, he and Giuseppina left for Paris. Although Verdi probably did not intend it at the time, he was to be based in France for the next two years. Paris was once again the capital of a monarchy, for Louis Napoleon, President of the Second Republic, had become the Emperor Napoleon III by a *coup d'état* and had begun to lead France into the industrial age. Verdi was fascinated by the new building work going on in Paris. He went out to the Bois de Boulogne to inspect the artificial lakes, and enjoyed watching the demolition of the slums between the Louvre and the Tuileries.

Antonio Somma thought he had gone to Paris to make arrangements for the production of *King Lear*, and Verdi was forced to point out to him that *Lear* would be 'too vast a subject and its forms too new and too daring to risk here, where all they understand are tunes that have been sung for the past twenty years'. By the end of the year (1853), the famous French playwright and librettist, the amazingly prolific Eugène Scribe, had produced his libretto for *Les Vêpres siciliennes*, which Verdi was to compose for production at the Paris Opéra as part of the celebrations for the Great Exhibition planned for 1855.

Verdi was now without doubt the most widely acclaimed living composer: Rossini had been silent for many years, Donizetti had died in 1848, and Wagner's operas (he had by then written *Der fliegende Holländer*, *Tannhäuser* and *Lohengrin*) had not been produced outside Germany. The Opéra considered itself fortunate to have commissioned Verdi's latest opera, and Parisian hostesses vied with each other to entertain the composer. The rumour which had floated back to Milan, that he was likely to 'put down roots' in Paris, was indignantly denied by Verdi: 'Put down roots? That's impossible. And, in any case, what would be the point of it? What purpose would it serve? Fame? I don't believe it. Money? I make as much, and perhaps more, in Italy. And even if I wanted to, I repeat, it's impossible. I'm too much in love with my desert and my own sky.' He claimed to have a fierce desire to return home, but he kept resolutely at work on *Les Vêpres siciliennes*.

Able in the past to work quickly, Verdi found he was progressing very slowly with his French opera. That he was composing a long, five-act work to a French text may have been a contributing factor, though Verdi's French was adequate to the task; what really held him up was that Scribe's libretto was hack-work in comparison with recent Italian librettos Verdi had set—and hack-work in a tradition alien to Italian opera, that of the five-act Meyerbeerian grand opera, filled with spectacle and with as much ballet as possible. The Paris concept of opera was diametrically opposed to the swift truthful drama which Verdi had brought into being in Italy, and Scribe's libretto made matters worse by reducing to absurd travesty an actual historical event, the Sicilian Vespers of 1282 in which the Sicilians had

Cover of the vocal score of Giovanna di Guzman, *a retitled version of Les Vêpres siciliennes.*

Sophie Cruvelli, who sang in the first production of Les Vêpres siciliennes.

massacred their French overlords. It was not until thirty years later, at the time of the posthumous première of a Donizetti opera, *Le Duc d'Albe*, that Verdi discovered Scribe had not even written an original libretto for him, but had adapted one he had already written in 1839 for *Le Duc d'Albe* which was not produced. That libretto, too, ended with a massacre. Scribe altered the names of the characters and some details of the plot, but the story is basically the same, and so is much of the actual dialogue! To Scribe's demented imagination, one massacre must have been very like another, and his story of the Spanish occupation of Flanders in the sixteenth century was easily turned into an account of the French occupation of Sicily in the thirteenth century.

Verdi did his best to adapt his musical and dramatic ideas to Parisian tastes, but his heart was not in the task. 'A work for the Opéra is enough to stun a bull', he wrote to a friend. 'Five hours of music. Phew!' He persevered with Scribe's inane hotchpotch, spending the winter months in Paris and the summer in the country at Mandres. By October he had completed four of the opera's five acts, and rehearsals were able to begin.

They did not continue for long, however, for after a few days the leading soprano, Sophie Cruvelli, disappeared. Cruvelli (originally Crüwell), a German soprano of twenty-eight and a popular favourite in Paris, was an attractive woman with a remarkably beautiful voice. She had sung Odabella in Verdi's *Attila* in Venice in 1847, a year after the opera's Venice première, and was thought to have been far superior to Sophie Loewe, the creator of the role. Cruvelli had been singing in Paris since 1851, and had appeared with immense success in *Ernani* at the Théâtre-Italien. Her sudden disappearance was widely publicized. She had been due to sing in Meyerbeer's *Les Huguenots* on the evening of 9 October, but had simply failed to appear. For more than a month nothing was heard of her. In London, where she was also popular, the Strand Theatre produced a farce, *Where's Cruvelli?* It seemed likely that the question would never be answered, when suddenly La Cruvelli reappeared, again without explanation. It was generally assumed, probably correctly, that she had taken it into her head to have an impromptu holiday with her lover Georges Vigier, whom she married two years later.

Rehearsals of *Les Vêpres siciliennes* were resumed; and none too soon, for Verdi had considered Cruvelli's disappearance the last straw, had asked the Opéra to release him from his contract, and was on the point of returning to Italy to work on *King Lear* for the opening of a new opera house in Genoa which the authorities wished to name after him. But the Opéra refused to release him, and rehearsals dragged on. Verdi's troubles with Scribe, with the management of the Opéra and with the whole Parisian concept of opera continued to increase, and on 3 January 1855 he wrote, in French, to the new director of the Opéra, Louis Crosnier:

Monsieur Crosnier,

I feel it my duty to let no more time pass without making a few observations concerning *Les Vêpres siciliennes*.

It is both upsetting and mortifying for me that M. Scribe will not take the trouble to improve the fifth act, which everyone agrees is uninteresting. I fully realize that M. Scribe has a thousand other things to concern him which are perhaps more important to him than my opera! But if I had been able to foresee his complete indifference I should have stayed in my own country where, really, I was not doing so badly.

I had hoped that M. Scribe would find it possible to end the drama with one of those moving scenes which bring tears to the eyes, and whose effect is almost guaranteed, since in my opinion the situation lends itself to that. Please note that this would have improved the entire work, which has nothing at all touching in it except the romanza in the fourth act.

I had hoped that M. Scribe would have been kind enough to appear at rehearsals from time to time, to be on the lookout for any unfortunate lines which are hard to sing, to see whether anything needed touching up in the numbers or the acts and so on. For example, the second, third and fourth acts all have the same form: aria, duet, finale.

Finally, I expected M. Scribe, as he promised me at the beginning, to change everything that attacks the honour of the Italians.

The more I consider this, the more I am persuaded it is dangerous. M. Scribe offends the French because Frenchmen are massacred; he offends the Italians by altering the historic character of Procida into the conventional conspirator beloved by the Scribe system, and thrusts the inevitable dagger into his hand. Good Lord, there are virtues and vices in the history of every race, and we are no worse than the rest. In any case, I am first of all an Italian, and whatever happens I will not become an accomplice in offending my country.

It remains for me to say a word about the rehearsals in the foyer. Here and there I hear words and remarks which, if not actually wounding, are at least inappropriate. I am not used to this, and I shall not tolerate it. It is poss-

The last act of I vespri siciliani *at La Scala, Milan, designed by Pier Luigi Pizzi.*

ible there are people who do not think my music worthy of the Opéra. It is possible there are others who think their roles unworthy of their talents. It is possible that I, for my part, find the performance and style of singing other than I would have wished! In short it seems to me, unless I am strangely mistaken, that we are not at one in our way of feeling and interpreting the music, and without perfect accord there can be no possible success.

You see that everything I have just said is serious enough for us to stop and consider how to avoid the catastrophe which threatens us. For my part, I see but one means and I do not hesitate to propose it: the dissolution of the contract. I quite realize you will answer that the Opéra has already lost some time and money, but that is little in comparison with the year I have lost here, during which I could have earned a hundred thousand francs in Italy. You will go on to say it is all very well to annul a contract when there is a deficit, to which I reply that I should by now have paid it if my losses and expenses here were not already too great.

I know you are too just and reasonable not to choose the lesser of the two evils. Trust my musical experience: under the conditions in which we are working, a success is really improbable. A half-success profits no one. Let each of us try to make up for lost time, try to arrange everything calmly, and we may both gain by it.

Accept, sir, the assurance of my great esteem.

PS. Excuse my bad French. The important thing is that you understand.

Again, the Opéra refused to release Verdi, and Scribe made none of the changes asked for. Rehearsals continued, unbelievably, for another five months, and the opera finally reached the stage on 12 June 1855. Ironically, it proved an immediate success with the Parisian public and also with the critics, one of whom wrote tactfully that 'Verdi's music has conformed to the procedure invented by French genius without losing anything of its Italian ardour'.

Les Vêpres siciliennes was given fifty performances at the Opéra during its first season, and was immediately produced in Italy, in an Italian translation by Verdi himself, who also made what slight changes were necessary to the vocal line. For cen-

sorship reasons, in Italy the opera was known variously as *Giovanna di Braganza*, *Giovanna di Guzman*, *Giovanna di Sicilia*, and even *Batilde di Turenna*, before it acquired its proper title, *I vespri siciliani*, six years later when Italy had finally become an independent nation. The opera held the stage in its Italian translation, and was given a new lease of life in German during the twentieth-century Verdi revival which began in Germany and Austria. In recent years there have been several productions in Italian and German, but there is a marked disinclination to give the original French version, even on the part of the Paris Opéra which in 1974 produced not *Les Vêpres siciliennes* but *I vespri siciliani*! The finest passages in the opera are those in which Verdi's sincerity of purpose burns through the dead-wood of Scribe's libretto. There are many of these, and the ballet music, a good half-hour of it, is delightful. But it is clear that Verdi's art, always concise and direct, was ill-suited to the prolix form and empty professionalism of Meyerbeerian opera.

Various business matters kept Verdi in Paris after the première of *Les Vêpres siciliennes*, in particular the problem of copyright. In order to prevent an unauthorized English production of *Il trovatore* he had hastened across from Paris to London while he was composing *Les Vêpres siciliennes*. Meanwhile, the House of Lords had passed a law decreeing that there could be no copyright protection for an opera written by a foreigner, unless the composer himself supervised the first production in England. This led Verdi to make another visit to London the following year, when he was advised to apply for citizenship either of Great Britain or of France who had various international agreements with England. But Verdi preferred to remain, as he put it, 'a peasant from Roncole, and I prefer to ask my government [the Duchy of Parma] to make an agreement with England'. Meanwhile he managed to prevent a Spanish impresario from presenting *Il trovatore*, *Rigoletto* and *La traviata* in Paris without payment.

At the end of 1855, he returned to Sant' Agata. The previous year he had told a friend that, of those operas of his which were out of circulation, there were two he would wish not to be forgotten: *Stiffelio* and *La battaglia di Legnano*. After consideration, he decided there was little he could do with *La battaglia di Legnano*, which had fulfilled its propaganda purpose. But he hoped to do something with *Stiffelio* by adapting it to a different libretto, and perhaps writing some new music for it. In March 1856, he wrote to invite Piave, who had provided the *Stiffelio* libretto, to Sant' Agata. Instructing him to bring some books or plays with him for consideration, he dismissed a suggestion Piave had made earlier: 'I have already mentioned to you that I would not like to make Stiffelio a crusader. Something newer and more interesting. Think about it.' And he added, 'Come quickly and, if you can, bring a lion ['leone', slang for poodle] with you, which you know will delight Peppina [Giuseppina].'

Piave arrived, but held out for his crusaders, and the eventual result was *Aroldo*, whose leading character is an English crusader. Meanwhile, Verdi went to Venice in March to conduct a revival of *La traviata* and, while he was there, agreed to write a new opera for the Teatro la Fenice, for production the following year. The subject he chose was another play by the Spanish playwright Antonio Garcia Gutiérrez, whose *El Trovador* had become *Il trovatore*. The new play, *Simon Boccanegra*, dealt with the historical character of that name, a fourteenth-century pirate who became Doge of Genoa. Piave was asked to prepare a libretto, working under the guidance of Verdi who himself planned the entire libretto, leaving his collaborator nothing but the task of turning it into verse. Work was interrupted while Verdi went on his travels again, to Paris and London, to protect his interests. While in Paris he supervised the French production of *Il trovatore*, for which he wrote ballet music and extended the finale, and continued to correspond with Piave about *Simon Boccanegra*. He was also in correspondence with the Teatro San Carlo in Naples concerning an opera for the 1857–8 season. *King Lear* was considered yet again, and casting was discussed. Verdi said he thought the Fool should be sung by a contralto, and Lear by a baritone. For Cordelia, he had in mind the soprano Maria Piccolomini, but the San Carlo could not procure her services, and Verdi refused to accept the soprano they offered in her place. He would not have singers foisted upon him, he said, 'not even if Malibran were to return from the grave'. Since he had himself sent a message to Maria Piccolomini assuring her that he would not be offended in the slightest if she refused the role, it would seem that, again, he was grasping at excuses to postpone tackling *King Lear*.

The usual trouble over censorship arose again with *Simon Boccanegra*, for the fourteenth-century Doge had been a man with the vision of a united Italy, and Verdi certainly intended his opera to portray the full horror of the fratricidal wars of the time. But he insisted that his libretto remain as he had conceived it, and this time he got his way. When he left Paris at the beginning of 1857 to return to Sant' Agata, he had by no means completed the opera. Dissatisfied with parts of Piave's libretto, he had asked Giuseppe Montanelli, a politician and former professor of law living in exile in Paris, to rewrite certain of the scenes. Montanelli complied quickly and competently, but when Verdi arrived in Venice in mid-February to rehearse, he still had one act to compose and the entire score to orchestrate.

Simon Boccanegra was produced at the Fenice in Venice on 12 March 1857, but failed to please its audience. One of the critics reproached Verdi for writing like Wagner, whose music he had still not heard. Verdi was disappointed with the opera's reception. 'I thought I had done something fairly good', he wrote, 'but it seems I was mistaken.' He had, in fact, written something more than fairly good, but it was taken up by very few other Italian theatres. Twenty-three years later Verdi was to return to it, and it is the thoroughly revised version of *Simon Boccanegra* which is performed today.

There were now only a few months before the première of the revised *Stiffelio*, now called *Aroldo*, which was to inaugurate the new opera house at Rimini in August. Verdi and Piave supervised the production, and Angelo Mariani, who was beginning to make a name for himself as an interpreter of Verdi, conducted the opera. *Aroldo* was even less successful than *Stiffelio* had been seven years earlier, though this was at first obscured by the excitement in the small town of Rimini about the opening of their new theatre and the presence in their midst of Italy's most famous composer. Until their final scenes, the plots of the two operas are virtually identical. *Stiffelio* was in three acts. Act III of *Aroldo*, whose hero is an English crusader, breaks off before the final scene of forgiveness in *Stiffelio*'s church, and substitutes an improbable Act IV set on the banks of Loch Lomond. The earlier acts take place in Kent or, to quote Piave's libretto, 'Egberto's castle near Kenth'.

John Shaw (baritone) *and David Ward* (bass) *in the 1966 Covent Garden production of* Simon Boccanegra.

Verdi now gave his full attention to the opera he had agreed to write for the 1857–8 season of the Teatro San Carlo, Naples, whose management had reluctantly agreed to a postponement of the *King Lear* project. At the time of the *Aroldo* première in August, the composer had not decided between Victor Hugo's *Ruy Blas*, another play by Gutiérrez entitled *El Tesorero del Rey Don Pedro*, and a libretto about Gustav III of Sweden, written a quarter of a century earlier by Scribe for Auber's opera, *Gustave III ou le bal masqué*. Verdi went so far as to have the Spanish play translated, and to abbreviate it for a librettist to versify, but by mid-September he had finally decided upon *Gustave III*, and Antonio Somma was entrusted with the task of translating Scribe's five-act French libretto into Italian, and recasting it in three acts.

When *Un ballo in maschera* eventually reached the stage, it was not in Naples in 1858, but in Rome in 1859. And it was no longer a story of the historical assassination of King Gustav III of Sweden at a masked ball in the Royal Opera House in Stockholm in 1792. Instead, it was about the fictitious British governor of an American colony. This came about through one of the oddest of Verdi's battles with the censors.

The historical Gustav III was an extremely colourful character. A nephew of Frederick the Great, he was, like his uncle, homosexual. Though he acquitted himself bravely in battle, he was considerably more interested in the arts than in war. He patronized artists and architects, wrote plays, and drew about himself a court of culture, elegance and learning. He possessed an intelligent agnostic's interest in theology, as well as an eccentric curiosity about the occult. He is said to have more than once consulted the famous Stockholm fortune-teller Madame Arvedson, who was a notorious intriguer as well as a foreteller of the future, and who figures in both Scribe's and Somma's librettos.

Scene from Simon Boccanegra *at La Scala*, 1972.

Gustav was twenty-six when he succeeded to the throne in 1772. He immediately antagonized the nobility by reducing their privileges in the process of enlarging his own, though he remained popular with the mass of the people. When he became king, he had been married for six years to Sophia Magdalena, Crown Princess of Denmark, though the marriage was purely one of expediency and the young king lived apart from his queen. In the words of a *Secret History of the Courts of Sweden and Denmark*, published early in the nineteenth century, 'dissolute company and perverted habits had deeply polluted his mind long ere the sceptre passed into his hand'.

Verdi's intention was to use the historical characters of Gustav, his assassin Count Ankarstroem, and the fortune-teller Madame Arvedson as portrayed in Scribe's libretto. Somma began work on the translation and adaptation; apart from a few matters of detail and the addition of the aria 'Eri tu', in which Ankarstroem reveals his motive for wanting to kill Gustav, Somma and Verdi stayed fairly close to Scribe, though they removed from their portrait of the king some of the French librettist's references to his intellectual and artistic aspects. They had been at work on the opera for some weeks when Verdi began to have doubts about the likelihood of the Neapolitan censors allowing the assassination of an historical reigning monarch to be shown on the stage. The more he thought about it, the less likely it seemed, although he had already submitted a prose synopsis of the plot. His fears were soon realized when his Neapolitan friend the critic Vincenzo Torelli confirmed that the authorities would not allow Gustav III to be portrayed on the stage.

Not altogether unprepared for this, Verdi replied that it would not be too difficult to transfer the scene elsewhere and change the names of the characters, although he would be sorry to have to lose the magnificence of Gustav III's court. At first, Somma seemed not to be especially worried by the censorship requirements. He wrote to Verdi:

A cartoon of Verdi confronting the censor over Un ballo in maschera.

the action from eighteenth-century Sweden to seventeenth-century Stettin, in Pomerania. It was not until Verdi had arrived in Naples in January 1858 that he discovered the censor had refused to allow the opera to proceed, with or without the changes in time and place. On 14 January, in Paris, a bomb had been thrown under the carriage of Napoleon III on his way to the Opéra, an incident which understandably increased the nervousness of the Neapolitan monarchy. Naples was, in any case, sufficiently aware of the danger of regicide, since in the previous year the reigning king had been attacked with a bayonet by one of his own soldiers. From Naples, on 7 February, Verdi broke the news to Somma:

> They began by objecting to certain phrases and words, and then entire scenes, and finally the whole subject. They made the following suggestions, but only as a special favour:
> 1. Change the hero into an ordinary gentleman, with no suggestion of sovereignty.
> 2. Change the wife into a sister.
> 3. Alter the scene with the fortune-teller, and put it back to a time when people believed in such things.
> 4. No ball.
> 5. The murder to be off-stage.
> 6. Omit the scene of the drawing of the name.
> And, and, and!!
>
> As you can imagine, these changes are out of the question, so no more opera. So the subscribers to the theatre won't pay the last two instalments, so the government will withdraw the subsidy, so the directors will sue everyone, and already threaten me with damages of 50,000 ducats. What hell!

They will allow us to set the opera anywhere in the north, except Sweden or Norway. Very well, but where? Let me have your views about this. To find a period that will justify a readiness to believe in witches, as requested by his lordship the censor, will not be easy. But I can see that it will be in our interests to submit. So tell me what you want, and whether you want the action to be laid in Hungary or Poland or somewhere else. If it's a question of a northern court, a Duke, and of placing it at a time when the conflict between pagan barbarians and Christian civilization was a real one, perhaps it would not be a bad idea to set it in Pomerania, which is a part of Prussia. It was an independent Duchy in the twelfth century, and the Teutonic knights were attempting to suppress the pagan ideas still extant in many parts of the country.

Verdi replied that he thought the twelfth century 'a little too remote for our Gustav', and far too raw and brutal a period. In his opinion they should look for 'some great prince or duke, a rogue whether of the north or not, who has seen something of the world and caught something of the atmosphere of the court of Louis XIV'.

Eventually, Verdi and Somma agreed to move

Although the opera was now completed except for the orchestration, the management of the Teatro San Carlo at this point prepared a completely different libretto in order to meet censorship requirements. It was called *Adelia degli Adimari*, and was set in fourteenth-century Florence. Verdi would have none of it and said so to the management, which immediately threatened him with legal action. Verdi and his solicitor issued a counter-claim against the theatre management,

Costume designs for Un ballo in maschera *at Covent Garden, 1975.*

the case was settled out of court, and an agreement was reached by which the contract was dissolved and Verdi was free to offer his opera elsewhere.

While the lawyers were still fighting, Verdi had in fact already offered the opera to the Teatro Apollo in Rome which accepted it, subject, of course, to the approval of the Papal Censor. In due course the Papal Censor approved both subject and plot, insisting however that the action be made to take place outside Europe. 'What would you say to North America during the English Colonial period?' Verdi asked Somma. And so King Gustav III of Sweden finally became Riccardo, Earl of Warwick and Governor of Boston, Massachusetts. That the libretto as we know it represents the final, though doubtless harassed, intentions of Verdi and Somma is confirmed by the amount of work they continued to do on it before the Rome première on 17 February 1859.

Verdi and Giuseppina arrived in Rome a month in advance, to find the city in a state of political excitement: there were rumours of imminent war between France and Austria, and the daughter of Vittorio Emanuele, King of Piedmont, was about to be married to a cousin of Napoleon III. Many people felt that the only future for the Italian states lay in a united Italy, probably under Vittorio Emanuele; they saw, too, that Verdi's name was an acronym for 'Vittorio Emanuele, Re D'Italia', Vittorio Emanuele, King of Italy. 'Viva V-e-r-d-i' was bandied all over Italy, painted on walls, displayed on banners and, in Northern Italy, shouted in defiance of the Austrians. In these circumstances, could the first night of *Un ballo in maschera* be anything other than a triumphant success? It would indeed have succeeded in any circumstances, for, unlikely as it may seem in view of its birth pangs, *Un ballo in maschera* is one of Verdi's middle-period masterpieces, a work whose characters are rich in humanity, whose melodies combine the warmth and vigour of the earlier Verdi with the lightness and elegance

101

which had entered his music with *La traviata*. In addition to the romantic drama, there is a great deal of laughter in the score of *Un ballo in Maschera*, ranging from the bright gaiety of Oscar the page, through Riccardo's amused irony, to the mocking taunts of the conspirators. Today, an increasing number of productions of the opera return to the first thoughts of Verdi and Somma, and change the locale and the characters' names back to those of late eighteenth-century Stockholm. In more than one such production the Swedish tenor Nicolai Gedda has brilliantly portrayed the historical Swedish monarch Gustav III.

The success of *Un ballo in maschera* was apparently not in any part due to the singers, for, in a letter to the Rome impresario some months after the première, Verdi referred to 'that wretched

Above: Italian patriots scrawling 'Viva Verdi' on a wall in Rome.
Right: Verdi leading a deputation to present a petition to Vittorio Emanuele II in 1859.

company you presented me with', and added: 'Put your hand on your heart and confess that I was a model of rare self-denial in not taking my score and going off in search of dogs, whose barking would have been preferable to the sounds of the singers you offered me.' Some weeks before the Rome première of *Un ballo in maschera*, *Simon Boccanegra* had been produced at La Scala, Milan, with a mediocre cast. The letter which Verdi wrote from Rome to his publisher Tito Ricordi when he heard of its failure is fascinating for the light it sheds on his attitude to the public, and the bitterness he still felt about the reception of his second opera nearly twenty years earlier:

102

The fiasco of *Boccanegra* in Milan had to happen, and it did happen. A *Boccanegra* without Boccanegra!! Cut a man's head off, and then recognize him if you can. You are surprised at the public's lack of decorum? I'm not surprised at all. They are always happy if they can contrive to create a scandal! When I was twenty-five, I still had illusions, and I believed in their courtesy; a year later my eyes were opened, and I saw whom I had to deal with. People make me laugh when they say, as though reproaching me, that I owe much to this or that audience! It's true that at La Scala, once, they applauded *Nabucco* and *I Lombardi*; but, whether because of the music, the singers, orchestra, chorus or production, the entire performances were such that they were not unworthy of applause. Not much more than a year earlier, however, this same audience illtreated the opera of a poor, sick young man, miserable at the time with his heart broken by a terrible misfortune [the death of his wife and two children]. They all knew that, but it did not make them behave courteously. Since that time, I've not seen *Un giorno di regno*, and I've no doubt it's an awful opera, but heaven knows how many others no better were tolerated and even applauded. Oh, if only the public at that time had, not necessarily applauded, but at least suffered my opera in silence, I shouldn't have been able to find words enough to thank them! If they now look graciously upon those operas of mine that have toured the world, then the score is settled. I don't condemn them: let them be severe. I accept their hisses on condition that I don't have to beg for their applause. We poor gypsies, charlatans, or whatever you want to call us, are forced to sell our labours, our thoughts, and our dreams, for gold. For three lire, the public buys the right to hiss or to applaud. Our fate is one of resignation, and that's all! But, whatever my friends or enemies say, *Boccanegra* is in no way inferior to many other operas of mine which were more fortunate: perhaps this one needed both more care in performance and an audience which really wanted to listen to it. What a sad thing the theatre is!!

Verdi and Giuseppina stayed on in Rome for some weeks after the first performance of *Un ballo in maschera*, and then returned to Sant' Agata for the summer. At the end of the summer, on 29 August, in an atmosphere of great secrecy, Verdi and Giuseppina Strepponi were married in the small town of Collonges-sous-Salève near the Swiss border of the province of Savoy. The legalizing of their union can have made little difference to their life, for they had been living together for the past twelve years. They brought a priest with them from Geneva to perform the ceremony, telling the local priest to 'go for a walk'. The ceremony was witnessed by two 'very distinguished persons', as Verdi described them in a letter written ten years later, 'the peasant and the carriage driver who took us from Geneva to Collonges'. It may be that Verdi and Giuseppina married because he had agreed to stand for public office and knew he was likely, within a few days, to be elected to the Assembly in Parma. He was duly elected in September, and was one of the small group deputed to carry the results of the Assembly's deliberations to Vittorio Emanuele in Turin. While in Turin Verdi met the great statesman Count Camillo Cavour, and it was Cavour who, when the unification of Italy was finally achieved in 1861, persuaded him to stand for election as the Busseto representative in the first Italian Parliament. The newly married Verdi spent the winter of 1859–60 in Genoa, and most of the following summer at Sant' Agata. When he was elected to Parliament, he and Giuseppina travelled to Turin in February 1861 for its opening by Vittorio Emanuele. Verdi was assiduous in his attendance at the sessions, but was no politician and contented himself with voting always as Cavour did. When Cavour died in June, Verdi organized at his own expense a memorial service in Busseto at which, as he wrote to his friend Count Arrivabene, 'the priest officiated without charge, which is quite something'.

With Cavour's death, Verdi's active interest in political life declined, and his thoughts turned again to composition. He refused to stand for re-election but finished his term of office, continuing

Giuseppina Strepponi at the time of her marriage to Verdi.

to attend the sessions in Turin regularly. While he was there, in the summer of 1861, he signed a contract to write an opera to be performed the following winter in Russia. The contract was with the Imperial Theatre, St Petersburg, and his first choice of subject was Victor Hugo's *Ruy Blas*. However, Hugo's play about a valet who becomes his Empress's lover and his country's prime minister failed to commend itself to the management of the theatre, whose decision was conveyed to Verdi by telegram with no reasons given, though presumably it was too democratic for the Tzarist régime. Verdi turned to other subjects, and finally decided upon a Spanish play he had considered once before: *Don Alvaro o La Fuerza del Sino*. Entrusting the libretto to Piave, he set enthusiastically to work on the opera which was to become *La forza del destino*.

The correspondence between Verdi and Piave reveals that the composer–librettist relationship was much as it had always been between them. Verdi harassed Piave, complaining frequently of the ugliness and incomprehensibility of his verses, but in due course the work was completed and Verdi and his wife set out for St Petersburg (Giuseppina making elaborate preparations for the journey and ordering large quantities of wine, pasta, cheese and salami to be sent on in advance). But as soon as they arrived in St Petersburg, the leading soprano of the opera became ill. There being no other singer suitable for the role of Leonora, Verdi asked to be released from his contract. Russia was bitterly cold, and the contrast between the luxury of the rich and the miserable condition of the poor distressed the Verdis. Giuseppina wrote to Count Arrivabene:

> ... One sees the cold but doesn't feel it. But, be quite clear, this curious contradiction is a benefit only to the rich who are able to shout 'Hurray for the cold, the ice, the sleighs and other joys of this world.' But the poor people in general, and the coachmen in particular, are the most miserable creatures on earth. Just think, dear Count, many of the coachmen stay sometimes all day and some of the night sitting still on their boxes, exposed to freezing cold, waiting for their masters who are guzzling in beautifully warm apartments while some of these unhappy beings are freezing to death. Such horrible things happen all the time. I shall never get used to the sight of such suffering.

The production of *La forza del destino* was postponed until the following autumn, and in February 1862 the Verdis left Russia. Verdi had reluctantly agreed to represent Italy at the London Exhibition of 1862, and to write a march for performance at the opening ceremony, so he and Giuseppina travelled by rail from St Petersburg to London. Having discovered that Meyerbeer (for Germany) and Auber (for France) were both writing orchestral pieces, Verdi decided to compose a short choral work for the occasion, and commissioned a text from the young composer and poet Arrigo Boito. Their *Inno delle nazioni* (Hymn of the Nations) for tenor, chorus and orchestra, a work lasting about fourteen minutes, was rejected by Michael Costa, the musical director of the exhibition, as not being in accordance with the terms of the commission. It is possible that Verdi's Hymn, which quoted from two famous revolutionary songs, 'La Marseillaise' and 'Fratelli d'Italia', was thought in some quarters to be dangerously republican. At that time, neither tune had become the national anthem of its country.

Verdi wrote indignantly to *The Times*, but immediately regretted it, for, his letter having revealed his Regent's Park address, the next day's post brought him an avalanche of letters with 'requests for autographs from all sides in a very odd and thoroughly English manner'. The *Hymn of the Nations*, an agreeable enough *pièce d'occasion*, was performed (though not as part of the official programme) at Her Majesty's Theatre on 24 May, Queen Victoria's birthday. It was received with great enthusiasm, and there were four more performances during the following week.

Verdi in 1859, the year in which he married Giuseppina Strepponi.

107

The Verdis returned to Sant' Agata, and in the autumn set out for St Petersburg once again. This time all went smoothly, and the opera was produced on 10 November 1862 (or 29 October according to the Russian calendar).

La forza del destino was enthusiastically received at its première. The Tzar and Tzarina attended the fourth performance and complimented Verdi in person, and the Tzar presented the composer with the Cross of St Stanislaus. At one of the performances there was a demonstration by student supporters of the Russian nationalist school of composers, but this merely had the effect of inciting the vast majority of the audience to more vociferous applause. Audiences and critics, of course, do not necessarily agree on the merits or defects of new works, and it is interesting to discover that the reviews in the Russian press by no means unanimously reflect the apparent enthusiasm of the St Petersburg

Cover of the Russian translation of La forza del destino *published in St Petersburg, 1862.*

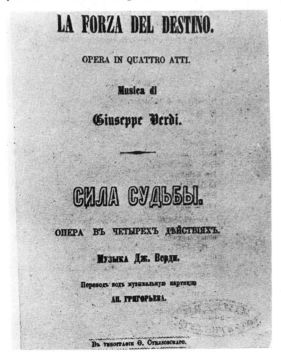

audiences. Four long and detailed reviews appeared in St Petersburg newspapers within days of the first performance. The only one which Verdi was able to read for himself was that printed in the French-language newspaper, the *Journal de St-Pétersbourg*, which, as it happened, was by far the most favourable, and of which Verdi sent a copy to his publisher in Milan. But the comments of the other three reviews did not find their way into print outside Russia.

That the première audience was enthusiastic can hardly be doubted. The critic of the *Journal* wrote immediately after the performance:

> It is midnight. We have just left the first performance of the new opera which Maestro Verdi has written expressly for the Italian Theatre of St Petersburg. We should not want this issue of the paper to go to press without mentioning the brilliant success of this beautiful work.
>
> We shall speak again at leisure about this magnificent score and about this evening's performance; but for the moment we wish to report the composer's victorious success and the ovations for the artists who, in order to comply with the insistent demands of the entire audience, had on several occasions to drag the celebrated composer on to the stage, to the sound of wild cheering and prolonged applause.
>
> It is our opinion that *La forza del destino*, of all Verdi's works, is the most complete, both in terms of its inspiration and the rich abundance of its melodic invention, and in those of its musical development and orchestration.

Three days later, the anonymous critic of the *Journal* published an essay of some five or six thousand words, in which he described and commented upon the opera in minute detail, with intelligence, sensitivity and open-mindedness.

The three other Russian reviews, though two at least were respectful, were less positive in tone than the *Journal*. The daily newspaper *Sin otechestva* (Son of the Nation) carried a review on 13 November (1 November, Russian calendar), signed M.R., which displayed a bias against Verdi as pronounced as the bias of the *Journal* towards him. 'A success it was', admitted the *Son of the*

Above: Verdi well muffled against the cold during his visit to St Petersburg in 1862.

Below: Verdi, seated next to the driver, takes a sleigh ride.

Nation, 'but by no means nearly as enthusiastic as certain wishful thinkers may have tried to make out.' Perhaps this is less indicative of bias concerning Verdi than of rivalry between the two papers, for the critic continued:

I have heard…that the telegraph wires of all Europe were humming with the news of the overwhelming and unprecedented success of Verdi's new opera. This is what our *Journal de St-Pétersbourg* also says, and though I shall probably be accused of being biased I cannot depart from my rule of speaking the truth unhesitatingly, even when it concerns a man of Verdi's stature. Regardless of those fawning critics who are always bowing and scraping and burning incense at the altars of the high and mighty, I shall come out boldly and say that the success was, as the French put it, *un succès d'estime.*

The other daily newspaper to review the première was the *Sanktpeterburgskiya vedomosti* (St Petersburg News). A different pair of eyes and ears, a different temperament, thus a different account of the audience reaction: 'The audience was the same as usual on first nights, though we also chanced to observe quite a number of faces rarely seen on any night…. Stray catcalls, also as usual, as the applause was not very clamorous.'

One further review appeared in the Russian press, in the weekly *Russki mir* (Russian World): it was by far the most unfavourable of the four. After criticizing Piave for the 'absurdity' of his libretto, the writer, J. Borodzich, turned to the music. Dismissing the first act as containing nothing of consequence 'because it consists only of recitative' (!) he was somewhat kinder to Act II, and then continued:

The third act begins with a short introduction, and then, after the curtain rises, a clarinet solo. The distinguished composer apparently included this sorry little solo for his fellow-countryman who plays in the opera orchestra, but he appears not to be a very good friend to judge by this solo. It failed to produce the

David Poleri as Alvaro in a Glyndebourne production of La forza del destino *at the Edinburgh Festival, 1951.*

slightest effect, even though it was also mentioned in the printed programme. Don Alvaro's aria, accompanied mostly by bassoon, and his duet with Don Carlo to the sound of trumpets, are both original. Next comes an absolutely artificial scene, a duet in which the mortally wounded soldier gets up, embraces his friend and begins to sing with all the vocal power at his disposal. Because of its expressiveness, Don Carlo's final aria engages the audience's full attention, but it is soon dispelled. The following chorus is extremely effective: joyous despite the minor key. The vivacious rataplan, sung to the sound of Preziosilla's drum, offers the audience a welcome respite after the lugubrious music which has led up to it, and in some ways it resembles *Les Huguenots.* There is nothing else in the third act worthy of note.

Act IV was a more serious disappointment to the critic of *Russki mir*. He has not even a good word for Leonora's great aria, 'Pace, pace, mio dio'; in fact, he has no words for it at all:

The public sits back and waits for the fourth and last act, in which most composers are touched by at least a fleeting moment of inspiration. But in this opera the wait proved to be utterly in vain. Except for the brief duet between the Father Superior and Fra Melitone, the fourth act is devoid of interest. The audience is presented with two murders and the death of Don Alvaro who jumps into the ravine.

This, of course, is not the ending of the opera as we know it. For the Milan production, seven years later, Verdi altered the St Petersburg ending, which had followed the original play by the Duke of Rivas, and substituted Alvaro's redemption through love, in the moving and compassionate trio which now brings to a quiet close Verdi's rich, sprawling, lovable essay on the respective values of the contemplative life and the life of action.

To call *La forza del destino* 'flawed', as some critics do, simply because it does not observe the Aristotelian unities is surely absurd. The opera covers a vast canvas, from the personal to the social, in the manner of Elizabethan theatre or the nineteenth-century novel: it is the work of a man

Left: Renato Capecchi and David Ward in La forza del destino, *Covent Garden, 1973.*
Above: Enrico Tamberlick (tenor), who sang in the first production of La forza del destino.

who has read Manzoni's *I promessi sposi*. The opera does not even deserve the other epithet that it has been given, 'uneven'. The emotions expressed in the military camp scenes are simple and banal, and so, frequently, is the music which portrays them. These glimpses of popular life perfectly complement, and indeed make their own implicit comment on, the personal drama. *La forza del destino* is not a flawed but a complex masterpiece. To us now, it appears to consist of a string of glorious arias, but in it Verdi was deliberately continuing his move away from strict aria form towards a greater fluidity and an apportioning of more orchestral and melodic interest to the recitative. He himself knew the kind of work he had composed. In a letter to his friend Vincenzo Luccardi, after the Rome production of 1863, he wrote: 'It's true that, in *La forza del destino*, the singers do not necessarily have to know how to manage *solfeggi*, but they must have soul, and understand the words and express their meaning.' Singers with 'soul' and understanding have, in recent years, revealed the opera as the valid work of music drama that it essentially is.

113

6 Maturity and Compassion: Don Carlos to Aida

From St Petersburg Verdi and Giuseppina travelled direct to Spain where, in January 1863, *La forza del destino* was to be produced in Madrid. It was also produced in Rome in the same month. After the Madrid première the Verdis spent several weeks in Spain, travelling mostly in Andalusia and visiting Seville, Granada and Cadiz. At Xeres, Verdi purchased a cask of sherry and had it shipped to Genoa to be forwarded to Sant' Agata. From Spain, the couple made their way to Paris, for Verdi had agreed to supervise a new production of *Les Vêpres siciliennes*. But he found the orchestral players listless and unwilling to rehearse. They played with exaggerated slowness a passage which he had criticized as being too fast, and then told him they considered they had rehearsed sufficiently and had other things to do. Verdi walked out. Back in Sant' Agata he returned to the cultivation of his fields, although he and Giuseppina from this time on began to spend their winters in Genoa, in a rented apartment with a view of the harbour.

For the Théâtre-Lyrique in Paris, where his *Macbeth* was to be staged in a French translation, Verdi agreed to compose ballet music. However, when he examined the score of the opera he had written seventeen years earlier, he found certain passages weak, 'or even worse, lacking in character', as he put it in a letter to his French publisher Léon Escudier. He listed what he considered needed to be done:

1. Write an aria for Lady Macbeth in Act II.
2. Various cuts to be reconsidered in the vision scene of Act III.
3. Completely rework Macbeth's aria.
4. Improve the first scenes of Act IV.
5. Write a new last act finale, deleting Macbeth's death scene.

In his correspondence with Escudier, Verdi made a number of detailed suggestions regarding the new production of *Macbeth*. He was especially concerned that the ballet should play its part in the drama, and not remain a mere *divertissement*:

> You will see that in the ballet there is a certain amount of action which fits very well with the rest of the drama. The apparition of Hecate, Goddess of Night, is appropriate, because she interrupts all the witches' dances with her calm and severe adagio. I don't need to tell you that Hecate must never dance, but simply mime. Also, needless to say, this adagio must be played by the *clarone* or bass clarinet (as is indicated), so that in unison with 'cello and bassoon it will produce a dark, hollow and severe tone in keeping with the situation. Please also ask the conductor to keep an eye on the dance rehearsals from time to time, to ensure that the dances remain at the tempi I have asked for. You know that dancers always alter the tempo. (At your Opéra, for example, they say the Tarantella can't be danced as I want it. But a child from the streets of Sorrento or Capua could dance it very well at my tempo.) If the tempi are altered, the witches' ballet will lose all its character, and will not produce the effect of which I think it capable.

Verdi worked on his revisions in the winter of 1864–5, and the opera was staged in Paris in April 1865. The Parisians did not find it greatly to their taste, and Verdi took particular exception to the critic who suggested that he did not know his Shakespeare. 'Oh, there they are greatly mistaken', he wrote to Escudier. 'It may be that I did not do *Macbeth* justice, but to say I do not know, I do not understand and feel Shakespeare, no, by God, no! He is my favourite poet, I have known him from my childhood, and read and re-read him continually.'

Although he did not travel to Paris in April to see the revised *Macbeth* staged, he and Giuseppina went there in the autumn and took an apartment on the Champs-Elysées, for Verdi had been asked to stage a revised *Forza del destino* in French and discuss the possibility of a new opera. The plan to produce the existing opera came to nothing: Verdi and the management of the Opéra could not reach agreement on several points, and Verdi had his doubts about the available singers. He was willing, however, to discuss possible subjects for a new opera to be composed in time for the next Paris Exhibition in 1867. Among the possibilities, *King Lear* raised its fearsome head again, and Verdi this time does appear to have given it serious consideration. He finally decided against *Lear* on the ground that, magnificent subject though it was, it would hardly be spectacular enough for the Paris Opéra. Instead, he agreed to compose an opera based on Schiller's play *Don Carlos*, to a libretto in French. An elderly librettist, Joseph Méry, who had worked with Auber, was entrusted with the task of adapting Schiller's great drama, but died before he had completed it. Camille du Locle, a young man who had recently written a libretto based on another Schiller play, was called in to finish *Don Carlos*, and when Verdi returned to Sant' Agata the following March he was able to take the libretto with him. He had, in fact, already begun to compose the music in Paris.

Verdi and Giuseppina returned home by sea via Nice and Genoa, and Verdi immediately immersed himself in the composition of *Don Carlos*, for the opera was due to have its première in November. Throughout April and May he worked continually, even allowing his farm workers to break in his foal Gisella, a task he would normally have undertaken personally. But in June the Austro-Prussian war broke out, in which Italy was marginally involved on the side of Prussia. The Italian generals refused to cooperate with one another, and suffered several defeats at the hands of the Austrians. A particu-

Verdi in 1867.

larly humiliating defeat for Italy was the battle of Lissa in the Adriatic, the first important naval encounter involving modern, steam-powered battleships. The Austrians with seven ships defeated the Italians with fourteen. By August Prussia had defeated Austria, but Italy considered itself dishonoured by the disastrous performances of its armed forces, and Verdi felt this so keenly that he asked the Paris Opéra to release him from his contract. The Opéra refused, and at the end of August the Verdis set out for Paris with four of the five acts of *Don Carlos* written. They spent some days at Cauterets in the Pyrenees, where Verdi completed the fifth act and took the hot sulphur waters for his psychosomatic sore throat.

Rehearsals began, but soon the usual Parisian

delays, including strikes, singers' illnesses real or imagined, and general indifference, all conspired to ensure a postponement of the première. Giuseppina filled in time by buying furniture for the apartment in Genoa while, as she wrote to a friend, 'at the Opéra they argue for twenty-four hours on end over such silly questions as to whether Faure or Marie Sax should raise their little finger or their whole hand'.

In the midst of all this, Verdi received the news that his father had died on 14 January 1867, at the age of eighty-two. *Don Carlos* was finally given a gala première at the Opéra on 11 March, in the presence of the Emperor and the Empress, and immediately afterwards Verdi left to deal with his family problems at Sant' Agata. The death of his father left him concerned about the future of

Left: A caricature of Verdi and Napoleon III after the first performance of Don Carlos *in Paris.*
Below: Verdi 'blowing his own trumpet' in the Requiem and Aida.

his eighty-three-year-old aunt and her seven-year-old granddaughter, both of whom had been living with his father.

Don Carlos was performed forty-three times at the Paris Opéra during the 1867 season, and the press notices it received were mainly favourable, though some critics again claimed to detect the influence of Wagner. (It should perhaps be stressed that Verdi had still to hear a Wagner opera; he had heard a performance of the *Tannhäuser* Overture in Paris the previous year and thought it 'mad'.) In Italy, Verdi's new French opera was produced in translation, as *Don Carlo*. Seventeen years later, when he and Boito were about to begin work on *Otello*, Verdi revised *Don Carlo* for a production in Vienna. When this was cancelled, he allowed the revised version to be performed at La Scala. He had made a number of changes, had composed some new music, and had deleted the entire first act, salvaging from it only a tenor aria which he

inserted into the former Act II. This four-act Italian adaptation is structurally less satisfactory than the five-act original version, and the latter is increasingly being preferred today, after nearly a hundred years in which only the 1884 revision was ever staged.

Schiller's great play *Don Carlos* is historically no more accurate than Shakespeare's histories are. In his search for poetic truth Schiller was willing to sacrifice mundane fact whenever necessary, as he did in his Joan of Arc play which Verdi had used for *Giovanna d'Arco* in 1845. His *Don Carlos*, though it deals with the Marquis of Posa's attempts to save Flanders from the despotic misrule of Philip II of Spain, is really a play of abstract ideas, a play about determinism and free will, and about the conflict between liberalism and religious obscurantism. In writing his opera, Verdi retained enough of his old revolutionary ardour to warm to the Marquis of Posa and his political idealism. Verdi was able to restore in music those qualities in Schiller which his librettists, in making a very long opera out of an even longer play, had necessarily to omit. Indeed, his opera adds an extra dimension to Schiller's text, a dimension achieved by a particular quality of Verdi's genius.

This quality is unaffected by considerations of the excellence or poorness of libretti. It must be admitted that, in many of Verdi's operas, the additional advantage gained by the music has to be offset by the loss of some characteristic peculiar to the play, which has not survived in the libretto. In *Ernani*, for instance, one gains Verdi's tuneful and dramatically apposite music, but loses the ironic humour which is a prominent feature of Victor Hugo's play.

Nevertheless in certain of Verdi's operas, over and above such considerations as to whether or not the play has been improved by its condensation into libretto form and length, an 'extra dimension' is created, not just by the addition of music, but by a quality that Verdi bestowed only rarely in music—that of compassion. For the most part, he maintains an impressive dramatic objec-

tivity: indeed Verdi is one of the most objective of composers, as opposed to his great contemporary, Wagner. But when Verdi does bestow compassion he does so generously, and always upon characters with whose plight he feels an immediate human sympathy, above and beyond the demands of the drama at that point. This element is something more specific than Verdi's humanity, his pessimism, his energy, all of which found frequent and magnificent expression through his heart-lifting melodic gift. When compassion enters Verdi's music, on certain rare, great occasions, it results in a special and distinct warmth of melody and orchestration which one

can hardly fail to recognize. There are early instances of this in *I due Foscari, Macbeth, I masnadieri* and elsewhere. Perhaps the most moving expression of this peculiarly Verdian accomplishment to be found in his operas before *Don Carlos* occurs in *Simon Boccanegra*, in the orchestral postlude to Fiesco's aria, 'Il lacerato spirito', where a tune of deep consolation is played by the strings, which one feels bathing not only Fiesco in its glow but oneself as well. Of course, other great composers of opera, Gluck, Mozart, Wagner and Richard Strauss, for example, have used their orchestra either to comment on the dramatic action or to reveal psychological truths

which it is not possible for the characters to express at that moment in their utterance on the stage. But Verdi's moments of compassion are more than this, and are all the more moving because of their rarity, and the discretion with which they are introduced. These are moments which are denied to the playwright, however great may be his eloquence, however real his humanity, for he has no direct means by which to comment on his characters. The novelist has an advantage over the playwright in this respect, and it is significant that the two novelists who most memorably express their concern for their characters in this way are the two great writers of the nineteenth century who have most in common with Verdi: Dickens and Dostoevsky. The Verdi opera whose form and whose juxtaposition of themes most easily calls to mind these novelists is *Don Carlos*, and the opera has an advantage over Schiller's play by virtue of its element of compassionate comment which, though it is manifest in one particular scene, emanates outwards from this scene to pervade the entire score. The scene in question is the *auto-da-fé* scene of the opera, which does not exist in Schiller's play.

Verdi's scene begins with a brassily martial orchestral introduction, and a festive chorus of great pomp. Then, a darker-coloured orchestral funeral march ushers in the procession of heretics condemned to die at the stake, while a monks' chorus chants about the day of reckoning. Their sickly, depressing monotone is immediately followed by a most beautiful tune played by the cellos, 'cantabile espressivo'. And suddenly it is as though Verdi himself has intervened to offer his comfort by way of secular benediction to the suffering victims of the church militant.

Throughout his life Verdi was concerned with writing music that was apposite and significant in terms of the given dramatic situation. But, at this moment, the music he writes is by no means in dramatic accord with the stage picture. The situation on the stage is grim: we have heard, and will continue to hear throughout this scene, music which is expressive of the pomp and terror of the *auto-da-fé*. Another composer, and in other circumstances—perhaps if the Grand Inquisitor were going to the stake—Verdi himself, might have used his orchestra to emphasize the external, dramatic point. But here he does not. Instead, what one is offered is a subjective comment by someone who has no real right to intrude—the composer in his own persona. And the tune, no more than a few bars, one musical sentence, wells up into one's consciousness from the cellos, and then dissolves before the harsh and sombre chant

of the exceedingly *un*compassionate Officers of the Inquisition.

Verdi never allowed his tunes to outstay their welcome, and the consoling melody vanishes, to reappear only once, appropriately, when the celestial voice is heard at the end of the scene. The tune is sung then by a solo soprano, accompanied by harp and harmonium.

Although it is heard only in the *auto-da-fé* scene, Verdi's compassionate melody spreads its influence much further afield, illuminating the dark recesses of Philip II's thoughts, the unhappiness of Elizabeth, the frenzy of Carlos, and the passionate jealousy of Eboli. *Don Carlos* is a complex work of art, and one emerges from a satisfactory performance of it with conflicting and disturbed feelings. It is, after all, one of the most richly rewarding operas one can encounter in the theatre, glowing with Verdi's humanity which he has been able miraculously to breathe into characters who, on the printed page of Schiller's play as the composer read it, must have seemed to him at first acquaintance to be frigidly formal.

Verdi had expected a much more enthusiastic reception for *Don Carlos* than the opera received, although it was greeted with respect wherever it was produced. Back at Sant' Agata, he devoted himself to work on the farm, while Giuseppina went to Milan to purchase more furniture and materials for the Genoa apartment. In Milan, she made the acquaintance of Verdi's lifelong friend the Countess Maffei, and the two women took to each other immediately. Through Clarina Maffei, Giuseppina met the great Italian poet and novelist Alessandro Manzoni, author of *I promessi sposi* (The Betrothed), which is probably still the most popular novel in the Italian language. Manzoni was also a great patriot and supporter of the liberal cause. When Verdi learned from Giuseppina that she had met Manzoni, his idol and, he once said, the only saint in his calendar, he was both delighted and envious. Giuseppina gave Verdi a photograph of Manzoni which he had in-

Alessandro Manzoni. A medallion by the sculptor Gaetano Monti.

scribed 'To Giuseppe Verdi, glory of Italy, from a decrepit Lombard writer', and, as Giuseppina wrote to Clarina Maffei, Verdi 'first turned red, then pale, and began to perspire...but more (and this is just between us), the very stern, proud bear of Busseto had tears in his eyes, and we were both so moved, so upset, that we sat there for ten minutes in complete silence.'

In the summer of 1867 Verdi's old benefactor Antonio Barezzi died in his eightieth year. The Verdis were by his bedside. Barezzi was weak and hardly able to speak, but he raised his eyes longingly to the piano which stood in a corner of his room. Verdi understood that the old man was asking to hear his favourite tune from *Nabucco*, so he sat and began softly to play the chorus of the captive Jews, 'Va, pensiero, sull' ali dorate'. Barezzi raised a hand, murmured 'O mio Verdi, mio Verdi', and died peacefully.

After the death of his father, Verdi and Giuseppina had taken into their home the seven-year-old Filomena Verdi, a grandchild of Verdi's uncle, and so his first cousin once removed. They educated the child, changed her name to Maria, and

considered her in every way as their daughter. The Verdis settled into a family routine in Sant' Agata and Genoa, though the year 1867 was not to end without a further disaster falling upon the family circle: in September Verdi's friend and librettist Piave suffered a paralytic stroke. Verdi wanted to go to him immediately in Milan, but Piave's wife advised him not to. Piave lingered on for eight years, unable to move or speak, during which time Verdi generously paid many of the family's expenses and settled an estate upon Piave's daughter. He also organized the publication of an album of songs for Piave's benefit, and bullied a number of composers, among them Auber, Mercadante and Ambroise Thomas, into contributing to it, as well as producing a song himself.

In the spring of 1868, Verdi visited Milan for the first time in twenty years (the distance from Busseto is no more than 80 miles), principally in order to meet Manzoni; he wrote later of 'the extraordinary, indefinable sensation' produced in him by Manzoni's presence. In the summer, a new opera house was opened in Busseto. Verdi had already had a number of quarrels with the Busseto Council concerning it, for he was annoyed by the Council's proposal to call it the 'Teatro Verdi', and even more annoyed by their assumption that he, now a fairly wealthy man, would contribute a large part of the building costs. At the theatre's opening ceremony in August *Rigoletto* was performed, preceded by an Overture, 'La Capricciosa', which, according to the programme, had been written by Verdi at the age of twelve. Everyone in the audience wore something green (*verde*), and when the curtain rose it revealed on the stage a bust of Verdi garlanded with flowers. But the composer's own box, given to him by the town, was conspicuously empty. He and Giuseppina had gone to a spa in the Apennines: they returned the day after the opera season ended.

In November, Rossini died in Paris. He and Verdi had never been close friends, but their acquaintance had been an amiable one. Verdi revered Rossini as a composer, and Rossini had

Verdi and Rossini.

once begun a letter to him, 'Rossini, ex-composer and fourth-rate pianist, to Verdi, distinguished composer and fifth-rate pianist'. Verdi now attempted to organize the leading Italian composers each to write one movement of a requiem mass, to be performed on the first anniversary of Rossini's death. A committee was set up in Milan, and the composers chosen. They were the most highly regarded composers of the time, after Verdi, but they are all virtually unknown today: Bazzini, Boucheron, Buzzolla, Cagnoni, Coccia, Gaspari, Mabellini, Nini, Pedrotti, Petrella, Platania and Ricci. Most, if not all, of these composers submitted their finished movements in good time, including Verdi who contributed the 'Libera me', but the difficulties in getting a chorus together proved, astonishingly, insuperable. The project foundered, and in due course the

composers had their manuscripts returned to them, to Verdi's bitter disappointment.

For a long time his publisher Ricordi had been urging Verdi to complete his revision of *La forza del destino*, and allow it to be staged at La Scala. Verdi was reluctant but, after the mayor of Milan had pleaded with him, and La Scala had agreed to engage the Czechoslovakian soprano Teresa Stolz, he gave his consent and even agreed to direct the rehearsals. His long boycott of La Scala was over, after twenty-four years. The revised *Forza del destino* was given a triumphant reception at La Scala in February 1869. Even the cautious composer referred to it the following morning as 'a decided success', adding that he thought Teresa Stolz and the tenor Mario Tiberini 'superb' and the orchestra and chorus 'divine'.

Camille du Locle, the librettist of *Don Carlos*,

Teresa Stolz, who sang in Verdi's Requiem.

had been corresponding with Verdi in an attempt to persuade him to write another opera for Paris. Various subjects were proposed by Du Locle (among them Molière's *Tartuffe*), but, in his letter turning down Du Locle's suggestion of *Froufrou* by Meilhac and Halévy, Verdi articulated his objections to the style of Parisian grand opera:

It's neither the fatigue of writing an opera nor the judgement of the Parisian public that prevents me; it's the certainty of never being able to have my music performed in Paris as I want it. It's very strange that a composer must always see his ideas altered and his concepts misrepresented. In your opera houses there are too many wise men (that is not meant to be an epigram). Everyone wants to pass judgement according to his own ideas, his own taste, and, worst of all, according to a system, without taking into account the character and individuality of the composer.... Thus, in the end, you have, not a work in one piece, but a mosaic. That may be fine, if you like it, but it's still a mosaic. You may reply that the Opéra has produced a string of masterpieces in this manner. They may be masterpieces, but allow me to say that they would be even more perfect if this pieced-together feeling and these adjustments were not so obvious at every point. No one, surely, will deny the genius of Rossini. All right, but, despite all his genius, his *Guillaume Tell* has about it this fatal atmosphere of the Opéra; and sometimes, although more rarely than in the work of other composers, you feel there's too much here, not enough there, and that it doesn't move with the honesty and security of *Il barbiere*. By this, I don't mean to disapprove of the way you work: I only mean to say that I really can't crawl once again under the Caudine forks of your theatres ... At the Opéra, after the first four chords you hear everyone whispering 'Ce n'est pas bon—c'est commun, n'est pas de bon goût. Ça n'ira pas à Paris!' What do such poor words as 'commun', 'bon goût', 'Paris' signify if you are dealing with a real work of art which should be universal?

The conclusion of all this is that I am not a composer for Paris. I don't know whether I have any talent or not, but I know for certain that my ideas of art are quite different from yours. I believe in inspiration, while you believe in

construction. For the purpose of discussion I admit your criterion, but I require the enthusiasm that you lack in feeling and in judgement. I want *art* in whatever form it is manifest, not *entertainment, artifice* and *the System*, which is what you prefer.

Despite those extracts, the general tone of Verdi's letter is not unfriendly. It ends with an invitation to Sant' Agata or Genoa, though Verdi can no longer guarantee the formerly splendid ravioli, 'for we no longer have our Genoese cook. Still, you won't die of hunger, and, what is certain, you will find two friends who think well of you and to whom your presence will be a real delight.' Du Locle persisted in his attempts to extract another French opera from Verdi, and suggested a play by the contemporary Spanish playwright López de Ayala. When he sent the Spanish play to Verdi, he enclosed a four-page synopsis of an Egyptian subject. It was this which aroused Verdi's interest. Rejecting the Spanish play, he praised the Egyptian synopsis and asked who had written it.

It was a question that, as will become apparent below, has not yet received a complete answer. Du Locle's immediate reply was that he himself had put it together from a story by the French Egyptologist, Auguste Mariette. Mariette, given the ennobling title of 'Bey' by the Khedive or Viceroy of Egypt in recognition of his achievements, had presented his story to the Khedive with the suggestion that it could form the basis of a really splendid opera to celebrate the opening of the Suez Canal. The Khedive agreed, and, through Mariette, Du Locle had been entrusted with the task of commissioning a famous composer to write the music. Verdi was the Khedive's first choice, followed by Gounod and then Wagner. When Verdi agreed to write the opera which became *Aida*, the Suez Canal had been open for several months. It might have been possible for the opera to have been written in time to inaugurate the new Cairo Opera House in November 1869, two weeks before the opening of the Canal, had

Costume design by Nicholas Georgiadis for the High Priest in the current Covent Garden production of Aida.

Du Locle been less mysterious in an earlier approach to Verdi, when he had asked the composer if he would be willing to write an opera for a far-distant country. At that time Verdi had refused, and the Cairo Opera opened with *Rigoletto*. Now that he had agreed to set Mariette's subject, a date for production was decided upon that gave him only six months to complete the opera. Du Locle drafted a complete libretto in French, but Verdi had decided the opera should be in Italian. Antonio Ghislanzoni, who some months earlier had worked on the revised *Forza del destino*, was hired to translate Du Locle's French text into Italian verse.

Verdi, as we have seen, had always played an active part in the shaping and writing of his libretti, and Ghislanzoni found that the composer was not easily satisfied. The correspondence between composer and librettist, which continued throughout the summer and autumn of 1870, reveals a great deal about Verdi's working methods. He was concerned to find not only the

right word for each phrase but also the most appropriate form for each scene. Dramatic effect was of enormous importance to him, yet he was never willing to sacrifice characterization to it. His comments and suggestions on the successive drafts sent to him by Ghislanzoni are always pertinent. Frequently they are more instruction than suggestion. Verdi was not impressed, for instance, with his librettist's first attempt at the second scene of Act I:

> To give you my honest opinion, I don't think this consecration scene has the importance that I was expecting. The characters don't always say what they should say, and the priests are not priestly enough. It seems to me that the right theatrical phrase is missing, or if it's there it's buried under the rhyme or the verse, and thus it doesn't leap out at one as it should. I'll write tomorrow, when I have read it over again quietly, and will tell you what I think should be done. I am convinced that this scene must have all the weight and solemnity possible.

In his next letter Verdi planned the shape and the action of Act II, Scene 1, in which Amneris is being dressed and adorned by her serving-maids. The following day found him again complaining that the *parola scenica* was lacking. 'I don't know if I can explain what I mean by "theatrical word",' he wrote, 'but I think I mean the word that most clearly and neatly brings the stage situation to life.' And he went on to suggest changes in the dialogue, all of them moves towards greater clarification and concision. Anticipating that Ghislanzoni would complain that his rhymes and his metre were being ruined, Verdi asserted that if the action called for it he would immediately abandon rhythm, rhyme and stanza. 'It is sometimes necessary in the theatre for poets and composers to have the talent *not* to write either poetry or music.' Rejecting Ghislanzoni's lines for a cabaletta, the composer wrote: 'I am not averse to cabalettas, but I must have a situation that gives a reason for them.'

Marina Krilovici as Aida and John Shaw as Amonasro in Aida *at Covent Garden.*

Verdi's requirements for the final scene were detailed and explicit:

At the end I should like to avoid the usual death agonies and not have the words 'I'm falling. I'm going before you. Wait for me. She is dead. I'm still alive, etc., etc.' I should like something sweet, other-worldly, a very short duet, a farewell to life. Aida should then fall calmly into the arms of Radames. Immediately, Amneris, kneeling on the stone of the vault, should sing a *Requiescant in pacem*, etc. I shall write the scene down to explain myself better.

FINAL SCENE

Radames:

> The fatal stone...forever
> Here is my tomb. The light of day
> I never more shall see.
> I shall never see Aida again.   (*Adjust this line*)
> Aida, where are you? May you at least
> Live happily, and my dreadful fate
> Never discover!...What is that moaning?
> Someone—A spirit?
> A vision? No, it's a human form.
> Heavens! Aida!...

(*These are just mixed-up words to be worked into beautiful verses by you. Similarly the following:*)

Aida:

> It is I.

Radames:

> You here? But how?

Aida:

> My heart anticipated your fate.
> I have waited here for three days.
> And here, far from all human sight,
> Close to you, I shall die.
> (*One more line*)

Radames:

> Die? You, so innocent
> Die? You?

(*Eight beautiful seven-syllabled lines for singing*)

Aida:

> Do you see? The angel of death,
> Radiant, approaches us
> To lead us to eternal bliss
> On his golden wings.
> Already I see the heavens opening

> There all pain will cease,
> There will begin the ecstasy
> Of everlasting love.

(*Singing and dancing from the interior of the temple by the priests and priestesses.*)

Aida:

> A sad song.

Radames:

> The celebration of the priests.

Aida:

> Our hymn of death.

Radames:

> Nor can my strong arms
> Move you, oh fatal stone.

Aida:

> In vain. For us, all is over. Hope is lost.
> We must die.

Radames:

> It's true. It's true.

> [*Duet*]

> O life farewell, earthly love
> Farewell, sorrows and joys...
> In infinity already I see the dawn,
> We shall be united forever in heaven.

(*Four beautiful twelve-syllabled lines. But, to make them suitable for singing, the accent must be on the fourth and eighth syllables.*)

Aida dies in the arms of Radames. Then Amneris, in deep mourning, enters from the interior of the temple and kneels on the stone above the vault.

> Rest in peace,
> Beloved soul...

When you have arranged this scene for me and have sent it, come to Sant' Agata two days later. By then I shall have written the music....

By the time Ghislanzoni's final draft arrived, however, Verdi had become impatient. He admitted that the librettist's verses were beautiful. 'But, since you were so late in sending them to me, I have written the music already, in order not to lose time, using the monstrous verses I sent you.'

So, as well as composing the music of the ethereal final duet 'O terra, addio', Verdi was also responsible for the '*versi mostruosi*', which are, in

Verdi and the cast of an early production of Aida *in Trieste.*

fact, anything but monstrous. They are simple, sincere and, in their context, extremely moving.

Until recently it had generally been assumed that Mariette's synopsis, which formed the basis of the libretto, was his own original work (although it is amusing to note that Mariette's brother claimed that his own unpublished novel *La Fiancée du Nil* had been plagiarized). But it now seems that earlier sources were also made use of, though whether by Mariette or by Du Locle is not certain. There are traces in the *Aida* libretto of both Metastasio's *Nitteti* and Racine's *Bajazet*, and the likelihood is that they were introduced by Du Locle in the process of expanding Mariette's idea into a full-length libretto.

Whoever may have had a hand in the libretto, the music emerged from Verdi alone—and in no more than four months. However, due to the Franco-Prussian war the shipping of the scenery from Paris to Cairo was delayed, and it was not until 24 December 1871 that *Aida* was given its first performance at the Cairo Opera House.

The opera was a triumph at its première and has remained immensely and deservedly popular ever since, though it has perhaps been somewhat misunderstood. It is generally thought of as a spectacular work, but, despite the spectacle of its triumphal scene (Act II, Scene 2), which is admittedly the grandest scene in the whole of grand opera, *Aida* is intrinsically an intimate opera. Much, indeed most, of the music for its three principal characters—Aida, Radames and Amneris—is scored with the delicacy and clarity of texture of chamber music. It is an opera about individuals and their passions, not about nations and their military exploits. It also has a strong claim to being Verdi's most original work for the stage, combining as it does the vigour and melodic fecundity of the composer's earlier period with something of the psychological penetration of the two masterpieces that were to follow (*Otello* and *Falstaff*) without in any way sounding like a transitional work.

From the beginning of the opera to the end Verdi's level of inspiration remains miraculously high. His command of the orchestra and ability to depict character in instrumental terms is complete and daunting. Even more daunting is the ease with which at the same time he contrives to write music that is as beautiful melodically and harmonically as it is dramatically apposite. This is a mastery Verdi acquired as early as *Macbeth*, a quarter of a century before, but nowhere is it more impressively displayed than in *Aida*. An example occurs in Act I, during the ensemble of 'Su! del Nilo', when, for eight bars, Radames has the martial tune while Aida sings a more agitated melody in shorter notes above it. This brief passage is quite remarkable, not only musically, for its shifting of the harmonic emphasis, but also dramatically, for the way it contrasts the situations of Aida and Radames: she hesitant and anxious, he exhilarated and determined. Another means of conveying the contrast in his characters' feelings, astonishing in its simplicity, is discovered by Verdi in the Amneris–Radames duet at the beginning of Act IV. Radames expresses his almost ecstatic anticipation of death in a tune of serene assurance, 'È la morte un ben supremo'. Amneris joins him only at the climax of the musical sentence, when she sings the same notes which display a deliberate melodic ambiguity. For her the phrase means desperation, for him determination.

The music of *Aida* makes no attempt at 'local colour'. Verdi created his own Egypt, just as surely as his beloved Shakespeare did in *Antony and Cleopatra*. He also wrote four superb roles for his singers, and in Amneris he created the finest of his magnificent series of mezzo-soprano characters.

Verdi did not travel to Egypt for the première of *Aida*. Instead, he took an active interest in the Milan production at La Scala, for which he wrote a full-scale Overture based on themes from the opera, to replace the short Prelude, and then decided against using it.

After the successful Italian launching of *Aida* in February 1872, Verdi spent the following months working on his farms, with occasional visits to supervise productions of his operas: to Parma for *Aida*, to Brescia for *La forza del destino*. At the end of the year he travelled to Naples to produce *Don Carlos* and *Aida*. Teresa Stolz was to sing in both operas, but shortly after the opening of *Don Carlos* she became ill, and rehearsals of *Aida* were postponed. Left with time on his hands at his hotel, Verdi composed a charming string quartet, and, a few days after *Aida* was at last staged, the quartet was performed at the hotel for a few friends.

In May of the following year Verdi's hero Alessandro Manzoni died at the age of eighty-nine. 'And with him', wrote Verdi to Clarina Maffei, 'ends the most pure, the most sacred, the highest of our glories.' The Catholic Church thought otherwise, and most of the newspaper obituaries were disguised attacks on the great novelist. Verdi was too upset to attend the funeral, but visited Manzoni's grave in Milan the following week. He also offered to compose a requiem mass for performance on the first anniversary of Manzoni's death, and to meet the expense of having the music printed, if the city of Milan would pay the costs of the performance. The mayor of Milan agreed, and Verdi began work on the mass during his summer holiday in Paris with Giuseppina. Its first performance was given in the Church of San

Above: Teresa Stolz as Aida in the first Italian production in Milan.
Right: Verdi conducting his Requiem in Milan.

Marco, Milan, on 22 May 1874, conducted by Verdi. It was a huge success, and three days later Verdi had to conduct a second performance at La Scala. Further performances in Milan were immediately arranged, and Verdi found himself obliged to take his Requiem on tour throughout Europe. He conducted seven performances at the Opéra-Comique in Paris, and a further eight the following year, 1875, when he was made a Commander of the Legion of Honour. There were four performances at the Vienna Opera, one of which was attended by the Emperor, who presented the composer with the medal of the Order of Franz Josef. The Requiem was greeted with wild applause, and Verdi was forced to repeat the Ricordare, Offertorium and Agnus Dei. While in Vienna, he also conducted *Aida* twice and attended a performance of Wagner's *Tannhäuser*. At the Royal Albert Hall,

A Milanese caricaturist's view of the first performance of Verdi's Requiem. The composer is seen with his four soloists.

London, he conducted three performances of the Requiem. No other requiem mass had ever been acclaimed in this manner, but then Verdi's Requiem is like no other requiem mass. Some critics complained that it sounded like an opera. It does, for it is a highly dramatic setting of the medieval Latin text, and could never be used liturgically. But it expresses the emotional meaning of that text as superbly as any one of Verdi's operas expresses the meaning of its libretto. Written for four solo singers, chorus and orchestra, the Requiem is an agnostic's interpretation of the drama of the day of judgement, magnificent in its intensity and in the compassion of its tragic view of the human condition.

130

7 The Last Years: Otello **and** Falstaff

The Czech soprano Teresa Stolz had sung the soprano part in Verdi's Requiem at its first performance and at most of the subsequent performances elsewhere in Italy and on the European tour. An ex-mistress of the conductor Angelo Mariani, she was an extremely attractive woman in her early forties. She had become a close friend of the Verdis, and there were persistent rumours about the exact nature of her relationship with the composer. The *Rivista Independente*, a journal published in Florence, ran a series of articles in 1875 depicting Stolz as a scheming and ambitious woman who deserted Mariani for Verdi, and purporting to describe a clandestine meeting between 'the amorous couple', Verdi and Stolz, in a Milan hotel room. Giuseppina was aware of the articles,

Giuseppina Strepponi in 1878.

and wrote a sympathetic and friendly letter to Stolz ('That we love you you know, you believe it, you rejoice in believing it, and you may be certain that towards you we shall continue the same as long as we live'). Whether there was a romantic attachment between the composer and the soprano whom he admired, it is impossible to know with certainty. Stolz's friendship with both the Verdis continued, and after Giuseppina's death she remained the composer's devoted friend in old age.

In 1876 Verdi produced *Aida* at the Théâtre-Italien in Paris, and the following year travelled to Cologne to conduct the Requiem. He refused, however, an invitation to return to Russia to conduct the Moscow and St Petersburg performances, although Teresa Stolz was to be the soprano soloist. It was at this time that his relations with the publishing firm of Ricordi became severely strained, for he had discovered irregularities in their accounts of money due to him. The more he investigated, the more alarming he found the situation to be, until eventually he sent for all his contracts with Ricordi, and those between Ricordi and the various theatres which had produced Verdi's operas, over a twenty-five-year period from 1851 to 1875. After examining all the books himself at Sant' Agata, Verdi came to the conclusion that the firm had been falsifying the accounts and cheating him out of royalties. He agreed to accept the huge sum of 50,000 lire from the firm, as compensation, though it was less than the amount really owed to him. He continued to do business with Ricordi, but complained bitterly that the firm had not only cheated him financially but also failed to uphold his interests, being concerned entirely with receipts from the theatres and not at all with the standards of production of his operas in those theatres.

From this time on, Tito Ricordi, with whom Verdi had done business for many years, began to be replaced by his son Giulio, who was in his thirties. It was Giulio Ricordi who persuaded Verdi to compose the masterpieces of his old age, for the composer, who was now in his sixties, talked as though his active career had come to an end with the Requiem. To Clarina Maffei, Verdi had written:

Are you serious when you speak of my *conscience obliging me to compose*?? No, no, you're joking, because you know better than I do that the account is settled. In other words, I have always conscientiously fulfilled the obligations I have undertaken, and the public has accepted my works with equal conscientiousness, with splendid hissing or applause etc. No one, then, has any right to complain, and I say again: 'Score settled.'

Verdi was perfectly happy at this stage to live the life of a farmer for several months of each year. When Maria Verdi, the young cousin whom he and Giuseppina had adopted, married Alberto Carrara, the son of Verdi's lawyer in Busseto, the composer himself gave the nineteen-year-old bride away. In the five years following the Requiem, Verdi wrote no music. But in 1879, when he and Giuseppina were in Milan where he was to conduct a performance of the Requiem in aid of the victims of the Po Valley floods, Giulio Ricordi and the conductor and composer Franco Faccio came to dinner at the Grand Hotel where Verdi always stayed in Milan. After dinner, Ricordi guided the talk round to possible opera subjects, to Shakespeare and, in particular, to *Othello*. Ricordi later said that, when he first mentioned *Othello*, Verdi's eyes focused on him with both interest and suspicion. Arrigo Boito, the composer and poet who had provided a libretto

The Théâtre-Italien in Paris, where many of Verdi's operas were produced.

133

for Faccio's Shakespeare opera, *Amleto*, was keen to collaborate with Verdi and to renew their acquaintance. Verdi had not seen Boito since they had met in Paris seventeen years earlier, when the young poet had written the text of the *Hymn of the Nations*. Reluctantly, he agreed to meet Boito again.

Verdi's reluctance was due not only to his lack of desire to compose another opera but also to the fact that, as a young man, Boito had written disrespectfully of him. But Boito was now in his late thirties and had become one of Verdi's most ardent admirers. Faccio brought him to the Grand Hotel the day after the dinner party, and the two men, one thirty years older than the other, found they got on remarkably well. Three days later, Boito showed Verdi his synopsis for a libretto based on *Othello*, and Verdi encouraged him to write the libretto: 'It will always be useful, whether for you, for me or for someone else.'

The Verdis returned to Sant' Agata, and Giulio Ricordi attempted to force the pace by suggesting that he and Boito should visit the composer to discuss further what they referred to as the 'chocolate idea'. But Verdi refused to be rushed into a commitment. He had recently begun to compose again, and had completed a *Pater noster* and an *Ave Maria* for performance the following year by the Milan Orchestral Society. Early in the new year, 1880, he travelled to Paris to stage and conduct *Aida* in French. Giuseppina advised Ricordi on how best to proceed with the 'chocolate idea' without frightening Verdi off the project. 'I think it best', she concluded, 'not to give him the slightest feeling that pressure is being applied. Let us allow the stream to find its own way down to the sea.'

Ricordi altered his tactics, and now proposed an easier, less complex, task: the revision of *Simon Boccanegra*, an opera which was hardly ever performed. Verdi was interested in doing something to rejuvenate his opera of twenty-three years earlier, and Boito agreed to make the necessary alterations to Piave's libretto. The two men set to

work, and within six months had produced the revised *Simon Boccanegra* which was performed at La Scala on 24 March 1881. This definitive 1881 version is the one performed today, and it includes a completely new scene added by Verdi and Boito to the 1857 opera, set in Boccanegra's council chamber. By the time of the *Boccanegra* première, Verdi and Boito found they had inadvertently passed the point of no return with Boito's Italian libretto, *Otello*, and were now fully committed to the project. During rehearsals of *Boccanegra* at La Scala, Verdi went so far as to promise the singer of Boccanegra, the French baritone Victor Maurel, that he would write for him the exacting role of Iago.

Verdi treated his new librettist with somewhat more respect than his earlier collaborators were accustomed to receive, but he was, to say the least, an active participant in the creation of the final draft of the *Otello* libretto, as this letter to Boito clearly reveals:

> I am in Milan, and your two letters were sent on to me here from Busseto. The finale is very well done indeed. What a difference between this one and the first! I shall add the four lines for Roderigo. Perhaps the other four for Desdemona will not be needed.
>
> It's so true that a silent Otello is grander and more terrible that my opinon would be not to have him speak at all during the whole ensemble. It seems to me that Iago alone can say, and more briefly, everything that must be said for the spectator's understanding, without Otello replying.

> IAGO: Hurry! Time is flying! Concentrate on your task, and on that alone. I'll see to Cassio. I'll pluck out his infamous, guilty soul. I swear it. You shall have news of him at midnight. (Altering the verses, of course.)

> After the ensemble, and after the words 'Tutti fugite Otello', it seems to me that Otello does not speak or cry out enough. He is silent for four lines, and it seems to me that (scenically speaking), after 'Che d'ogni senso il priva', Otello ought to bellow one or two lines: 'Away, I detest you, myself, the whole world!'

Verdi with Francesco Tamagno, the tenor who sang Otello in the first production, photographed at the Tuscan spa of Montecatini.

And it seems to me too that a few lines could be spared when Otello and Iago remain together:

OTELLO: But I cannot flee from myself. Ah, the serpent.

IAGO: Signor!

OTELLO: To see them together, embracing. Accursed thought. Blood, blood. The handkerchief. (*He cries, and faints.*)

IAGO: My poison is working.

OFFSTAGE CRIES: Long live the hero of Cyprus!

IAGO: Who can stop me from stamping my heel on that brow?

OFFSTAGE CRIES: Glory to the Lion of Venice!

IAGO: Here is the Lion!

A strangled cry on the word 'fazzoletto' [handkerchief] seems to me more terrible than a commonplace exclamation like 'O Satana'. The words 'svenuto', 'immobil' and 'muto' somewhat hold up the action. One stops to think, and here it's a case of hurrying on to the end. Let me have your opinion.

I haven't finished. The chorus has little or nothing to do. Could one not find a way of moving it about a bit? For example, after the words 'In Cyprus, my successor is to be—Cassio!' Chorus, with four lines not of revolt but of protest: 'No, no, we want Otello!'

I know perfectly well that you will reply at once: 'Dear Signor Maestro, don't you know that nobody dared to breathe after a decree of the Serenissima, and that sometimes the mere presence of the Messer Grande sufficed to disperse the crowd and subdue the tumult?'

I would dare to rejoin that the action takes place in Cyprus, the Serenissima were far away, and perhaps for that reason the Cypriots were bolder than the Venetians. If you come to Milan, I hope to see you. I'm not sure, but I think you have all the poetry of the third act.

The work proceeded, slowly and with interruptions. Verdi did not begin actual composition of the opera until March 1884, after he had revised and shortened *Don Carlo* for a production at La Scala in January of that year. And when he did begin, he wrote spasmodically, short bouts of intense creativity alternating with periods of neurotic inactivity. By early October 1885, he had finished composing and was ready to begin scoring and revising, which was to occupy him for a further year. It was not until December 1886 that Verdi was able to tell Boito that the final pages of *Otello* had been sent off to the firm of Ricordi.

The première at La Scala, Milan, followed soon after, on 5 February 1887. For weeks before that date the excited anticipation of the Milanese public had been steadily brewing. Verdi and Giuseppina came to Milan early in January, when the seventy-three-year-old Verdi coached the singers and took the first orchestral rehearsals. The actual

Gwyneth Jones as Desdemona and James McCracken in the title-role in Otello *at Covent Garden.*

performances were conducted by Boito's friend Franco Faccio, and the first night was an absolute triumph. Blanche Roosevelt, an American singer who was present in the audience, described the reception accorded the performance:

> The ovations to Verdi and Boito reached the climax of enthusiasm. Verdi was presented with a silver album filled with the autographs and cards of every citizen of Milan. He was called out twenty times, and at the last recalls hats and handkerchiefs were waved, and the house rose in a body. The emotion was something indescribable, and many wept. Verdi's carriage was dragged by citizens to the hotel. He was toasted and serenaded; and at five in the morning I had not closed my eyes in sleep for the crowds still singing and shrieking 'Viva Verdi! Viva Verdi!'

Otello is widely regarded as Verdi's greatest opera, though to debate priorities at Verdi's level of achievement is an almost pointless exercise. What of *Falstaff*, still to come? What of *Rigoletto, Don Carlos, La traviata*? And they are not the only serious contenders. With *Otello*, however, two old, mutually contradictory charges against Verdi were finally laid to rest: on the one hand, that he was a skilful popular melodist whose orchestral composition was devoid of interest, and, on the other, that in his more recent operas he had taken to imitating Wagner. Verdi's handling of the orchestra in *Otello* is masterly, but it owes nothing to Wagner. The drama is firmly in the hands of the singers; nevertheless, the end of the long path along which Verdi had been guiding Italian opera for nearly half a century, away from the old set forms and towards a fluid, continuous dramatic melody, had at last been reached. That a man in his seventies should have composed so fresh and inspired an opera as *Otello* is miraculous, but finally irrelevant. *Otello* is a great work because it conveys the drama of Shakespeare's play in musical terms, because the psychological acumen of its musical characterization is so penetrating, and because it conveys with such accuracy that combination of tenderness, violence and sensuality typical of the Elizabethan age, and yet it achieves this in music which is not archaic, indeed not bound to any particular period. The language of *Otello* sounds as direct to us today as it did to Verdi's Milanese audience nearly a century ago. Freed from the harmonic constrictions of his early works and able to range where it will, Verdi's melody places itself wholeheartedly at the service of the drama and yet remains recognizable as melody. The influence of this one opera by Verdi upon twentieth-century opera is immense by comparison with that of the only other indisputable genius of nineteenth-century opera, Richard Wagner. Wagner's path has proved a *cul-de-sac* to other composers, for the operas of Wagner produced only imitations before their quasi-symphonic style ceased to be heard in the opera house. But the works of Verdi, and *Otello* in particular, have led to the operas of Puccini and Britten, and to the main stream of operatic composition today. A work of art can be original while yet revealing clearly its line of descent from the past (for example, *Rigoletto*, *Il trovatore*, *La traviata*). *Otello*, however, betrays the influence of no other composer.

Verdi and Giuseppina stayed in Milan for the first three performances of *Otello*, and then left to go to their apartment in Genoa. A few weeks later, Verdi was at work on his farm. Before he left Milan, La Scala had begged him to write another opera, but he preferred, he said, to go back to being the peasant of Sant' Agata. *Otello* began to travel the rounds of Italian theatres, and when Franco Faccio, who had conducted the Scala première, conducted the opera in Brescia in the summer and wrote to the composer of its success, Verdi replied ironically: 'Well, then, *Otello* is making its way even without its creators?!! I had got so used to hearing people proclaim the glories of those two [Tamagno and Maurel] that I was almost persuaded they had written this *Otello*. Now you deprive me of any illusions by telling me that the Moor is going well without these stars! Can it be possible?'

Boito had been at work on a French translation of *Otello*, and brought it to Verdi at Sant' Agata in the autumn. He was keen to collaborate on another opera, but Verdi managed to turn the conversation to Boito's own music. *Nerone*, with libretto and music both by Boito, had been on the stocks for some time (and was still not finished

when Boito died more than thirty years later), and Verdi enjoyed asking the composer if his librettist was holding him up, or vice versa. Verdi spent the winter of 1887–8 in Genoa, and the following spring at Sant' Agata supervising the construction of a hospital he was building nearby at Villanova for the benefit of the community; he preferred now to live the life of a private citizen with a social conscience and sufficient wealth to indulge it. His hospital was opened in November 1888, and is still functioning today.

Verdi's concern for his local community did not stop with the provision of a hospital. Observing that many farm workers were drifting from the country to the towns, he attempted to combat this in his own vicinity by reducing the rents on his farms, improving many of the properties and introducing a new irrigation system. At the beginning of 1889, he was annoyed to hear that plans were being made to commemorate the fiftieth anniversary of the production of his first opera, *Oberto*, and he wrote irritably to Giulio Ricordi in an attempt to stop anything from being done. However, he was unable to prevent La Scala from performing *Oberto* on the anniversary date, 17 November, and could express his disapproval only by staying at home in Sant' Agata, where he was flooded with congratulatory messages.

Knowing Verdi's devotion to Shakespeare, and that, ever since the failure of *Un giorno di regno* in 1840, he had wanted to compose another comic opera, Boito cleverly sent the composer the synopsis of a libretto called *Falstaff*, based on Shakespeare's *The Merry Wives of Windsor*. Verdi read it immediately, was delighted with it, and wrote to Boito to say so and also to criticize two or three points of detail. Then, as though suddenly realizing that he was in danger of committing himself too precipitately, he wrote again the following day pointing out the obstacles. He was an old man, he did not want to overtax his

*Verdi and Arrigo Boito at Sant'Agata, with (*inset*) the note which Verdi scribbled to Boito when he had finished work on* Otello.

strength. What if he could not finish the opera? And what about Boito's own *Nerone*? But Verdi failed to sustain the note of caution he was attempting to sound. At the end of the letter his delight at the prospect of composing *Falstaff* burst forth: 'So let's think about it (and take care to do nothing that would interfere with your own career), and, if on your side you can find a reason, and I find some way of casting ten years from my shoulders, then what joy to be able to say to the public:

Here we are again!!
Come and see us.'

Boito hastened to remind Verdi that he had been longing to find a good comic opera libretto all his life, and that the only way to end his career more splendidly than with *Otello* would be with *Falstaff*. 'I don't think you will find writing a comic opera fatiguing', he urged. 'A tragedy makes its composer really suffer, for his mind dwells on grief and his nerves become unhealthily agitated. But the jests and laughter of comedy exhilarate both mind and body.'

Verdi needed no further persuasion. 'Amen, and so be it', he replied. 'Let us then do *Falstaff*. Let's not think of the obstacles, my age and illnesses.' He added, however, that he wanted to keep secret the fact that they were at work on the opera. He had a fear of arousing expectations which he might not be able to satisfy. Boito completed his libretto and Verdi began to set it, but for months not even Giulio Ricordi was let in on the secret. Verdi tried to keep up the fiction that he was writing the opera purely 'to pass the time', and refused to discuss plans for its production. He even told Ricordi he thought it would be seen to better advantage at Sant' Agata than at La Scala.

Verdi worked slowly on *Falstaff* throughout 1890. In November, he was distressed by the death in Paris of his old friend and pupil, Emanuele Muzio, and for a time was too upset to go on with his comic opera. But he did go on, despite his seventy-seven years, his increasingly frequent moods of depression, and occasional interruptions. He continued the composition of *Falstaff* throughout the following year, but told Ricordi that he was still not willing to think about the eventual staging of the work:

When I was young, despite ill-health I was able to stay at my desk for ten or twelve hours, working constantly. More than once, I set to work at four in the morning and continued until four in the afternoon, with only a cup of coffee to sustain me, working without a break. I can't do that now. In those days, I was in command of my health and my time. Now, alas, I am not. So, to conclude: the best thing to say now and in the future to everyone is that I cannot and will not make the slightest suggestion of a promise in connection with *Falstaff*. If it is to be, it will be, and it will be as it is to be!

In April of the following year, Verdi interrupted work on the opera to go to Milan to conduct the orchestra of La Scala on the hundredth anniversary of the birth of Rossini. It was the last time he was to conduct an orchestra in public. By September he had completed *Falstaff*, and was able to send the last act to Ricordi, with a note of sad farewell to the character of Falstaff scribbled on the score, beginning 'Tutto è finito. Va, va, vecchio John'. (It's all finished. Go, go, old John.)

Having now completed the opera, Verdi was willing to agree to its production at La Scala. He and Giuseppina travelled to Milan immediately after New Year's Day, 1893, and he began to rehearse *Falstaff*, sometimes for as long as eight hours a day. His colleagues were amazed by the vigour of the composer, who was now in his eightieth year; two famous neurologists commented in print upon his extraordinary physical condition and mental resilience, and another published an article entitled 'The Psychological Phenomenon of Verdi'. The première of *Falstaff* was set

Three views of Falstaff: Tito Gobbi at Covent Garden, with (inset left) costume design by Jean-Pierre Ponnelle for Glyndebourne, 1976, and (right) the French baritone Victor Maurel in the first production at La Scala in 1893.

for 9 February, and excitement mounted in Milan several days in advance as music critics began to arrive from all over the world. The first performance was conducted by Eduardo Mascheroni, as Boito's friend Faccio, who had conducted *Otello*, had died while Verdi and Boito were at work on *Falstaff*. The opera was given a wildly enthusiastic reception, and Verdi, leading Boito on stage to share the applause, was recalled countless times. Finally, the Verdis and Boito escaped from the opera house by a side exit to avoid the crowd at the stage door, arriving at the Grand Hotel only to find another cheering crowd which refused to disperse until Verdi had appeared on the balcony of his suite three times.

From its very first performance, *Falstaff* was greeted with delight, not unmixed with astonishment that an opera of such life-enhancing warmth and joyous lyricism could have been produced by an octogenarian. The character of Falstaff himself is perfectly observed, and the composer's affection for him pervades the entire score. Some of the other characters are presented almost as Jonsonian 'humours', but as such they are immensely effective. Alice Ford is a key role, and a year after the première Verdi wrote to advise the director of the Opéra-Comique in Paris, where *Falstaff* was about to be performed in French: 'Pay great attention to the role of Alice. First of all, of course, it needs a beautiful and very agile voice, but, most important, it needs an actress of personality, with a little of the devil in her. The role of Alice is not developed as much as that of Falstaff, but it's as important from the stage point of view. It's Alice who leads all the intrigues of the comedy.'

One of the most striking aspects of the opera is its melodic fecundity. The tunes follow one another so breathlessly that it is as though Verdi, in extreme old age, had tapped a new source of inspiration. Paradoxically, it is the sheer profusion of melody in *Falstaff* that has occasionally led the casual hearer to suppose the opera less tuneful than early Verdi, for there is little time for the tunes to be assimilated as they fly past: the tempo in general is extraordinarily brisk, and it is not until the beginning of the final scene that there comes a moment of repose. *Falstaff* is an opera of wit, wisdom and good humour which seems to pass in a sudden flash of inspiration, a magical transformation of the pot-boiler that Shakespeare wrote to order for Elizabeth I.

The cry went up for another Verdi opera. Boito suggested a third Shakespeare play, *Antony and Cleopatra*, and even tried to tempt Verdi finally to make his assault upon *King Lear*, but it gradually became evident that, although he intended to continue composing music, the likelihood of Verdi producing another full-scale opera was extremely slight. He made some revisions to the score of *Falstaff* in time for its French première in April 1894, which he attended with Giuseppina. For the production of *Otello* in French in the autumn he composed ballet music to be inserted into Act III, and stipulated that it should be performed in precisely five minutes and fifty-nine

OSPEDALE G. VERDI

142

seconds! Despite his age, he returned to Paris for the *Otello* première, at which the French President presented him with the Grand Cross of the Legion of Honour. He and Giuseppina spent the winter of 1894–5 in Genoa, but also visited Milan where Verdi conferred with Camillo Boito, an architect and elder brother of Arrigo. At Verdi's instigation, Camillo Boito had drawn up plans for a rest home in Milan for aged musicians, a project which occupied the composer a great deal in his last years. Verdi had acquired the site five years earlier, and was now free to give his undivided attention to this generous and imaginative project. Treating his architect in the same manner in which he used to treat his librettists, Verdi interfered throughout the building process, insisting on private bedrooms instead of dormitories, and making a number of other improve-

Left: The hospital founded by Verdi to serve his local community is still functioning today.
Below: The rest home for old and impoverished musicians in Milan, endowed by Verdi.

ments. He began, slowly, to compose again: a *Te Deum* and a *Stabat mater*. The latter was to be his last finished work.

Giuseppina's health had been failing for some months, and in the autumn of 1897 she was forced to take to her bed with bronchial pneumonia. She appeared to recover, but then suffered a relapse, and died on 14 November at the age of eighty-two. Verdi, who was with her at the end, was deeply distressed to lose his life's companion, the only one who had known him since before the première of his first opera, nearly sixty years earlier. Depressed and alone, he concentrated on finishing his *Stabat mater* and on supervising the construction of his Casa di Riposo per Musicisti, paying frequent visits to the building site. He took care to set up a foundation to manage the Home, which is still in operation today, known to all in Milan as the Casa Verdi. In addition to providing the building, Verdi bequeathed to the foundation a large sum of money in Treasury bonds, his credit with the firm of Ricordi amounting to two

hundred thousand lire, and all the royalties from his operas.

Three of Verdi's sacred pieces, the two recently composed and a *Laudi alla Vergine Maria* of ten years earlier, were performed in Paris in Easter Week, 1898, and Boito wrote from Paris of their successful reception. Verdi now divided his time between Sant' Agata, Genoa, the Grand Hotel in Milan, and the spa of Montecatini where he submitted with resigned good humour to being gaped at by crowds as the 'grand old man of Italian music' whenever he ventured forth in public. He was less good-humoured when the Milan Conservatorium sought his permission to change its name to the Verdi Conservatorium. He refused, observing to his friends: 'They wouldn't have me young; they shan't have me old.'

In July 1900 the assassination of King Umberto shocked the whole of Italy. The Queen was moved to write a prayer, and Verdi attempted a musical setting of it, for which a few sketched phrases are all that exist. But his musical imagination was no longer functioning, and in any case he found the deep religious feeling of the Queen's words 'so primitive and true that music would seem pompous and artificial beside them'. When he was sent a versification of the prayer, Verdi replied that he would not even attempt to compose anything for the rhymed version, which he thought lacked the sincerity and spontaneity of the Queen's original words.

Verdi spent the Christmas of 1900 in Milan, where he visited Maria Carrara-Verdi his adopted daughter, his old friends and colleagues Boito and Teresa Stolz, and his publisher Giulio Ricordi. Maria Carrara-Verdi later recalled that, at Sant' Agata, after the death of Giuseppina, Verdi would sometimes sit at the piano playing the sad aria of Philip II from *Don Carlos* in which the King imagines himself in the long and lonely sleep of death.

Early in January, Verdi wrote from Milan to

The elderly Verdi in his garden at Sant'Agata.

a friend in Genoa: 'Even though the doctors tell me I am not ill, I feel that everything tires me. I can no longer read or write. I can't see very well, my feeling grows less, and even my legs don't want to carry me any more. I'm not living, I'm vegetating. What am I doing still in this world?' A few weeks later, on the morning of 21 January, his physician paid a routine call on the composer at the Grand Hotel, and found him quite well. Later the same morning, however, as he was dressing, Verdi suddenly lost consciousness and fell back on to his bed. The doctor was recalled, and discovered that a cerebral haemorrhage had paralysed his entire right side. For some days Verdi lay in a coma. The news of his collapse had quickly spread through Milan, anxious crowds waited outside the hotel for news of him, and straw was laid in the street to deaden the noise of traffic. At precisely ten minutes to three on the morning of 27 January 1901, Verdi died peacefully. He was eighty-seven.

'I wish my funeral to be extremely simple and to take place either at daybreak or at the hour of the Ave Maria, without either music or singing. Two priests, two candles and a cross will be sufficient', Verdi had instructed his principal heir, Maria Carrara-Verdi. As far as was possible, his wishes were respected. However, as he was laid to rest beside Giuseppina in the Milan municipal cemetery early on the morning of 30 January, people in the crowd, standing at a distance from the small group of family mourners, wept. A voice from among them began to sing quietly, 'Va, pensiero, sull' ali dorate', and was soon joined by others. A month later, the coffins of Giuseppe and Giuseppina Verdi were removed to the now completed Casa di Riposo, as Verdi had requested, and a state ceremony was made of the occasion. Two hundred thousand people lined the black-draped streets of Milan to say farewell to their beloved hero, wreaths arrived from all parts of the world, and the performance of 'Va, pensiero' was this time a scheduled one, sung by a choir of eight hundred conducted by Arturo Toscanini.

Something of warmth, of passionate energy seemed to have left the world with Verdi, and the world mourned.

The finest artists are not always the most admirable of human beings, nor do the most upright and honourable of men necessarily turn out to be possessed of superlative artistic talent. But Verdi was a great composer and a great man. It could not have been easy in early nineteenth-century Italy for a child from a poor family to step out of his class, to make the most intelligent use imaginable of the meagre education available to him and to supplement it by his own curiosity about the world, yet Verdi managed to achieve this. In the process, he managed also to retain his humanity and warmth throughout a long life, which is surely even more difficult, and to act honourably and fairly. He was a creature of moods, and could often be gruff and testy in manner; he was also temperamentally inclined towards melancholy, a sceptic and a pessimist. But his gift for friendship was real, and survived many trials. His loyalty to his friends and to the standards of behaviour he set himself never faltered. He worshipped no god but greatness in man: his god was Shakespeare, his only saint Manzoni. His enemies were hypocrisy, mediocrity, pretentiousness and the clergy. With Shakespeare he shared a humanistic philosophy, and that natural and instinctive compassion for mankind which, though it may be felt by many artists, can be infused into their creative work by so few.

In 1951, on the occasion of the fiftieth anniversary of Verdi's death, the great English opera composer Benjamin Britten wrote these words about

Verdi's funeral in Milan, 1901.

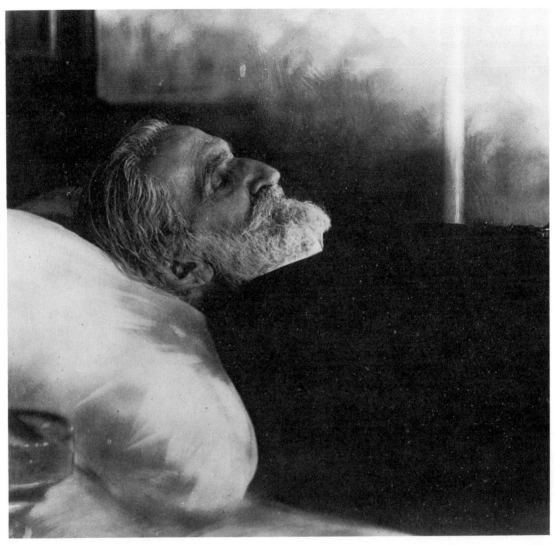

Verdi on his deathbed in the Grand Hotel, Milan.

the colossus of Italian opera: 'I am an arrogant and impatient listener; but in the case of a few composers, a very few, when I hear a work I do not like I am convinced it is my own fault. Verdi is one of those composers.'

Let the final tribute be Stravinsky's: 'Verdi! Verdi! the great, the mighty Verdi. How many beautiful things there are in his early works as well as in the final ones. I admire him unconditionally, a truly great composer! I prefer Verdi to all other music of the nineteenth century.'

Verdi's Life in Brief

1813   Verdi born, 10 October
Lives in Busseto, studies music
Rejected by Milan Conservatorium, studies privately in Milan
Commissioned to write opera for Teatro Filodrammatico

1836   Marries Margherita Barezzi, 4 May

1837   Begins to write *Oberto*. Daughter Virginia born, 26 March

1838   Son Icilio born, 11 July. Virginia dies, 12 August

1839   Icilio dies, 22 October. *Oberto* performed at La Scala, 17 November

1840   Margherita dies, 18 June. *Un giorno di regno* performed at La Scala, 5 September

1842   *Nabucco* performed at La Scala, 9 March

1843   *I Lombardi* performed at La Scala, 11 February. *Ernani* commissioned by Teatro La Fenice, Venice

1844   *Ernani* performed at La Fenice, 9 March. *I due Foscari* performed at Teatro Argentina, Rome, 3 November. Verdi produces revival of *I Lombardi* at La Scala, 26 December

1845   *Giovanna d'Arco* performed at La Scala, 15 February. Verdi breaks off relations with La Scala. Travels to Naples for première of *Alzira*, 12 August

1846   *Attila* performed at La Fenice, 17 March. Nervous exhaustion; six months' rest

1847   *Macbeth* performed in Florence, 14 March. Travels to London for première of *I masnadieri*, 22 July

1848   *Il Corsaro* performed in Trieste, 25 October

1849   *La battaglia di Legnano* performed in Rome, 27 January. Lives in Paris with Giuseppina Strepponi. Returns to Busseto with Strepponi. Travels to Naples for première of *Luisa Miller*, 8 December

1850   *Stiffelio* performed, Trieste, 16 November

1851   *Rigoletto* performed at La Fenice, 11 March. Returns to Paris with Strepponi for winter

1853   *Il trovatore* performed in Rome, 19 January. *La traviata* performed at La Fenice, 6 March

1854   In Paris, composing *Les Vêpres siciliennes*

1855   *Les Vêpres siciliennes* performed at Paris Opéra, 13 June

1857   *Simon Boccanegra* performed at La Fenice, 12 March. Produces *Aroldo* at Rimini

1858   Quarrels with Neapolitan censorship

1859   *Un ballo in maschera* performed in Rome, 17 February. Verdi and Strepponi married, 29 August

1861   Elected to the first Italian parliament

1862   *La forza del destino* performed in St Petersburg, 10 November

1867   *Don Carlos* performed at Paris Opéra, 11 March

1868   Meets Manzoni in Milan

1869   Opening of Suez Canal, and of Cairo Opera House with *Rigoletto*

1870   Verdi agrees to write opera for Cairo

1871   *Aida* performed in Cairo, 24 December

1873   Death of Manzoni. Verdi composes Requiem in his memory

1874   Requiem performed in Milan, 22 May

1879   Verdi and Boito agree to collaborate on revision of *Simon Boccanegra*

1881   Revised *Simon Boccanegra* performed at La Scala, 24 March. Verdi and Boito begin work on *Otello*

1887   *Otello* performed at La Scala, 5 February

1889   Fiftieth anniversary of *Oberto*; revival at La Scala, 17 November. Verdi and Boito begin work on *Falstaff*

1893   *Falstaff* performed at La Scala, 9 February

1897   Death of Giuseppina, 14 November

1901   Death of Verdi at Grand Hotel, Milan, 27 January

Major Compositions

(The dates in brackets are those of first performances)

Operas

Oberto (1839)

Un giorno di regno (1840)

Nabucco (1842)

I Lombardi (1843) (French version, *Jérusalem*, 1847)

Ernani (1844)

I due Foscari (1844)

Giovanna d'Arco (1845)

Alzira (1845)

Attila (1846)

Macbeth (1847) (revised version, 1865)

I masnadieri (1847)

Il corsaro (1848)

La battaglia di Legnano (1849)

Luisa Miller (1849)

Stiffelio (1850) (revised version, *Aroldo*, 1857)

Rigoletto (1851)

Il trovatore (1853)

La traviata (1853)

Les Vêpres siciliennes (1855)

Simon Boccanegra (1857) (revised version, 1881)

Un ballo in maschera (1859)

La forza del destino (1862) (revised version, 1869)

Don Carlos (1867) (revised Italian version, *Don Carlo*, 1884)

Aida (1871)

Otello (1887)

Falstaff (1893)

Choral works

Inno delle Nazioni (1862)

Messa da Requiem (1874)

Quattro Pezzi Sacri (1898, ii to iv only)

 (i) Ave Maria

 (ii) Stabat mater

(iii) Laudi alla Vergine Maria

(iv) Te Deum

Chamber music

String Quartet in E minor (1873)

Further Reading

Abbiati, Franco, *Giuseppe Verdi*. Milan, 1959.

Budden, Julian. *The Operas of Verdi* (Vol. 1). London, 1973.

Cesari, Gaetano and Luzio, Alessandro (eds), *I Copialettere di Giuseppe Verdi*. Milan, 1913.

Gatti, Carlo, *Verdi*. Milan, 1931; English translation, London, 1955.

Godefroy, Vincent, *The Dramatic Genius of Verdi*. London, 1975.

Martin, George, *Verdi, His Music, Life and Times*. London, 1965.

Osborne, Charles, *The Complete Operas of Verdi*. London, 1969.

Osborne, Charles (ed.), *Letters of Giuseppe Verdi*. London, 1971.

Pougin, Arthur, *Verdi*, trans. James E. Matthew. London, 1887.

Sheehan, Vincent, *Orpheus at Eighty*. London, 1959.

Toye, Francis, *Giuseppe Verdi: his Life and Works*. London, 1931.

Walker, Frank, *The Man Verdi*. London, 1962.

Index

Author's Acknowledgements

The extract on pp. 16–20 from Verdi's fragment of autobiography is taken from Pougin's *Verdi* (see Bibliography), in the translation by James E. Matthew.

I should like to thank Messrs Victor Gollancz Ltd for allowing me to incorporate certain passages from *The Complete Operas of Verdi* and *Letters of Giuseppe Verdi*.

Picture Acknowledgements

The publishers would like to thank the following for supplying illustration material: Bildarchiv Preussischer Kulturbesitz p. 87; Glyndebourne Festival Opera pp. 48/49 (Guy Gravett); The London Coliseum pp. 76 (Anthony Crickmay), 78; Museo Teatrale alla Scala pp. 6, 12, 14 (below), 44, 54, 72, 74 (below), 80, 81, 82, 92, 109, 116, 122 (below), 132/3, 145; Harold Rosenthal pp. 23, 28, 29, 35, 39, 50, 52, 61, 67, 71, 72, 94, 96, 97, 98, 110; Royal Opera House pp. 76 top (Donald Southern), 85 top (Chris Arthur), 101 (Donald Southern), 112 (Reg Wilson), 118/19 (Houston Rogers), 119 inset (Donald Southern), 124, 125 (Donald Southern), 136 (Reg Wilson), 141 (Donald Southern); Weidenfeld & Nicolson Archives pp. 2, 10, 19, 74 (top), 81, 102, 122, 129, 130, 131, 135, 139, 144, 146; Welsh National Opera p. 64 (Alfred Evan); Reg Wilson pp. 83, 84, 85 (below), 86, 87 (below), 88.